As editorial director of  oversaw the creation of bestsellers on subjects to cookery, from DIY t consumption at the Dige on blurb writing. **Vic Mayhew** was Northern editor of the *Daily Mirror* and had a spell in the Republic of Ireland as editor of the *Irish Star*. He was appointed by Rupert Murdoch to oversee the launch of Murdoch's first newspaper in the USA. As night editor of the *Sun*, he wrote that newspaper's style guide.

£1.50

A MISCELLANY FOR WORD LOVERS

Origins, Meanings and Quizzes

Robin Hosie and
Vic Mayhew

Constable & Robinson Ltd
55–56 Russell Square
London WC1B 4HP
www.constablerobinson.com

First published in the UK by How To Books,
an imprint of Constable & Robinson, 2014

A copy of the British Library Cataloguing in Publication Data
is available from the British Library

ISBN: 978-1-84528-515-9 (paperback)
ISBN: 978-1-47211-015-2 (ebook)

1 3 5 7 9 10 8 6 4 2

Printed and bound by
CPI Group (UK) Ltd, Croydon, CR0 4YY

Contents

QUICK QUIZZES

SIGNS OF THE TIMES

EXPLORING THE LANGUAGE

Introduction

HOW TO USE THIS BOOK

First and foremost, *A Miscellany for Word Lovers* is meant for everybody who wants to build a fuller, more powerful and more persuasive vocabulary. It sets out to do this by making learning fun. Words that may at present be well out of reach, a little way beyond reach, or so close that they are on the tip of your tongue are presented in more than 100 quizzes. Could you, with total confidence, use such words as nidifugous, solipsistic, evanescent, atavistic, autochthonous, misericord, hagiography, parameter, stagflation, internecine and eclectic? Some of these words, possibly, but *all* of them?

Most of the quizzes – carrying the heading **WHAT'S THE WORD?** – begins with crossword-style descriptions of words that share a common theme – geology, the atmosphere, volcanoes, earthquakes, collective names for birds (a murder of crows... a murmuration of starlings... an unkindness of ravens...), the language of science and so on. If a little help is needed, the crossword theme is continued by clues that give the first few letters of the target word. The **ANSWERS** help to fix newly acquired words in the mind by giving their origins, using the words in sample sentences and, when it is helpful, offering memory-jogging tips.

Interleaved between the quizzes are entries that explore the oddities, quiddities and curiosities of the English language. To list just a few, **SIGNS OF THE TIMES** entries draw attention to the links between the turmoil of historical events and the growth of the English vocabulary. Entries under the heading **DIVIDED BY A COMMON LANGUAGE** turn the spotlight on differences between American English and British English. Example: An American who promises to be with you momentarily means that he will be there in a short time – not for a short stay. **MOVIE MEMORIES** and **QUOTE OR MISQUOTE?** are short quizzes that test the memory and at the same time are reminders of just how powerful and effective words can be.

The way to get the best out of *A Miscellany for Word Lovers* is to set yourself a target: to add one new word to your working vocabulary every day, every week, every month or at any other rate that appears reasonable and, above all, is achievable. The book can be dipped into at any page for a quick consultation, or read from cover to cover, according to personal preference.

Happy word searching!

Robin Hosie and Vic Mayhew

Words About Words

A   Long-winded language that makes its point in a roundabout way.

B   Unnecessary repetition, using different words but saying what has already been said.

C   The use of words that are surplus to requirements.

D   A question that is asked for the sake of effect and so does not call for an answer.

E   Using the wrong word to comic effect while the correct meaning is clearly understood.

F   The transposition of initial letters in spoken words, producing an entertaining result, as in: *You have hissed all my mystery lectures and tasted the whole worm.*

G   The use of words that echo the sound of the object or action they describe, as in *sniffle, babble, chortle,* and in such comic-book words as *SPLAT! POW!* and *OUCH!*

H   The replacement of a word or words, usually by dots, so that the meaning, though not spelled out, is implied.

I   An impressive word for what are usually termed brackets, or an aside from the main topic when making a speech.

Clues

A   14 letters: *cir-----------*

B   9 letters: *tau------*

C   8 letters: *ple-----*

D   2 words, 10 letters and 8: *rh-------- q-------*

E   11 letters: *mal--------*

F   10 letters: *spo-------*

G   12 letters: *ono---------*

H   8 letters: *el------*

I   11 letters: *par--------*

See page 2 for answers

Answers, Word Origins and Usage

A **Circumlocution**. Latin *circum* (round) + *loqui* (to speak). Example: I'm not sure at this present time that I entirely agree with you on the question you recently raised about whether it might or might not be a good idea to consider the need to bring back capital punishment.

B **Tautology**. *Adj*: **tautological**. From Greek *tautos* (identical) + *logos* (word).

C **Pleonasm**. *Adj*: **pleonastic**. Example: These two last jigsaw pieces will complete the puzzle, because they fall into place nicely.

D **Rhetorical question**. Example: We all know what the government can do with its offer of 75p a week, don't we?

E **Malapropism**. After Mrs Malaprop, a character in Richard Sheridan's 1775 comedy *The Rivals*, who had an entertaining way of attaching the wrong meaning to words as in: She's as headstrong as an allegory instead of as an alligator.

F **Spoonerism**. After the Revd William Spooner (1844–1930), warden of New College, Oxford, whose verbal tic caused much amusement among colleagues and undergraduates.

G **Onomatopoeia**. From the Greek for 'name' and 'make', so making the name match the sound of what is named, as in *cuckoo*. The accent falls on the penultimate syllable, so that the word sounds rather like *on a mat appear*.

H **Ellipsis**. From the Greek for 'falling short'. Example: We don't want to fight, but by jingo, if we do…

I **Parenthesis**. From a Greek word meaning 'putting in alongside'.

Signs of the Times

New words do not arrive out of thin air. They enter the language naturally, out of the events and circumstances of their times; and they give an insight into the nature of the society that produces them.

Celts and Romans

The Romans invaded Britain in AD 43, overran the Celts and did not leave until early in the fifth century, when Rome itself was threatened by Barbarians. Ding the centuries of Roman rule even the lowliest of Britons must have acquired at least a working knowledge of Latin, but the hardiest linguistic survivors from the Roman period are to be found among place names. Those ending in *-castle*, *-caster* and *-chester* are derived from the Latin *castrum* (castle, fortress). Among other Roman survivals are Britannia, Hibernia and Caledonia.

The language of the Celts is preserved in place names, in features of the landscape and in present-day Welsh. Oddly, Welsh is not a Welsh word. It stems from the Anglo-Saxon *wealas*, meaning 'foreigners'. The Celts called themselves *Cymri* and their land *Cymru*, a name echoed in that of the county Cumbria and sung with fervour whenever the Welsh rugby team line up for an international match. Place names that end in *-dunum* (hill) and its variants *-down* and *-don* are likely to be Celtic, as are those containing *pen* (head or hill), as in Penrith. *Crag* and *combe* are Celtic in origin, as are the names of a number of rivers, including the Thames, Severn and Trent.

At War with the Language

The following job advertisement is an example of the kind of gobbledegook that seems to have an appeal to bureaucratic minds. In attempting to sound impressively official it misses what should be its main aim: clarity.

> The decision has been taken to appoint a consultant change manager who, supported by their own consultant team will be engaged full time...for a continuous 6–9 month period to deliver change management services in respect of the authority's strategic procurement function and exchequer management services...to deliver a corporate procurement function able to better exploit modern procurement techniques and technologies...The overall objective is to improve the existing centralised model needed to access substantial price savings and introduce process efficiencies.

Apart from the shaky grasp of grammar (*a* manager supported by *their* own team) the use of **deliver** in this job advertisement by the change management services is enough by itself to cause a shudder. Postmen deliver letters, boxers deliver left hooks, judges deliver verdicts, but the verdict on those who speak of delivering services is: Guilty! The offence is repeated in *deliver a corporate procurement function*. What on earth does that mean? And what is wrong with using the word *provide*? The closing sentence of the job advertisement, although there is a meaning buried in it somewhere, is management gobbledegook at its finest.

Words About Words

A A compulsive tendency to talk in a torrent of words that may not make sense.

B A terse manner of speaking, with not a word wasted.

C Steeped in sorrow, as in a sad poem or song.

D A public tribute, usually to somebody who has recently died.

E Praise that is particularly lavish. Example: *Every time you speak, your wit and charm light up the room.*

F Praise that is intended to reach a wide audience.

G Extremely talkative, sometimes to the point of being tiresome.

H Words spoken or written in conclusion, often as a means of summing-up.

I The use of a polite term in place of one that is considered vulgar or offensive.

Clues

A   10 letters: *log-------*

B   7 letters: *la-----*

C   5 letters: *e----*

D   6 letters: *eu----*

E   8 letters: *enc-----*

F   9 letters: *pan------*

G   10 letters: *loq-------*

H   10 letters: *per-------*

I   9 letters: *eu-------*

See page 6 for answers

Answers, Word Origins and Usage

A **Logorrhoea**. Greek *logos* (word) + *rhoia* (flow). Memory-jogger: diarrhoea.

B **Laconic**. Laconia was a name for ancient Sparta and once, when an enemy warned the Spartans, *'If I enter your city I will raze it to the ground'*, the laconic reply was: *'If!'*

C **Elegy**. *Adj*: **elegiac**. Greek *elegos* (a sorrowful poem). Memory-jogger: Gray's *Elegy Written in a Country Church-Yard*.

D **Eulogy**. *Adj*: **eulogistic**. From a Greek word meaning 'praise'.

E **Encomium**. From a Greek word meaning 'high-flown speech in praise of a conqueror'.

F **Panegyric**. Greek *pan* (all) + *agora* (an assembly).

G **Loquacious**. *Noun*: **loquacity**. Latin *loqui* (to speak). Example: John was so loquacious when somebody brought up the subject of income tax that we all thought he had either been severely overcharged in the past or was seriously underpaying in the present.

H **Peroration**. Latin *per* (to the end) + *orare* (to speak).

I **Euphemism**. *Adj*: **euphemistic**. Greek *eu* (well) + *phanani* (to speak). Example: Does anybody need to visit the bathroom before we sit down to eat?

Words About Words

A   Long-winded; packed to the point of tedium with unwanted details.

B   Showing courteous respect and a readiness to yield.

C   To speak or act without rehearsal or apparent preparation.

D   Criticism that is bitter and destructive.

E   A word or phrase that reads the same way backwards or forwards.

F   Words intended to sway opinion, especially when moral decisions have to be made.

G   A vigorous way of putting the argument for or against a question that is under dispute.

H   An actor's monologue, or lines addressed to the audience rather than to characters on the stage.

I   Descriptive of a sound that falls pleasantly on the ear.

Clues

A   6 letters: *pr*----

B   11 letters: *def*--------

C   11 letters: *ex*---------

D   8 letters: *di*------

E   10 letters: *pal*-------

F   8 letters: *did*-----

G   9 letters: *pol*------

H   9 letters: *sol*------

I   7 letters: *eup*----

See page 8 for answers

Answers, Word Origins and Usage

A **Prolix**. *Noun*: **prolixity**. Latin *prolificus* (many offspring).

B **Deferential**. *Noun*: **deference**. Latin *deferre* (to submit).

C **Extemporise**. *Adj* and *Adv*: **extempore**. Latin *ex tempore* (out of time). Example: The director encouraged his actors to extemporise because he believed that following a script too closely killed spontaneity.

D **Diatribe**. Latin *dia* (completely) + *tribein* (to rub out).

E **Palindrome**. *Adj*: **palindromic**. Greek *palin* (back, again) + *dromos* (running).

F **Didactic**. From a Greek word meaning 'skilled in teaching'.

G **Polemical**. *Noun*: **polemic**. Greek *polemos* (war). Example: In the days when *The Times* was known as *The Thunderer*, its leading articles denounced overseas atrocities with polemical fervour.

H **Soliloquy**. *Verb*: **soliloquise**. Latin *solus* (alone) + *loqui* (to speak). Example: Poor Charles – his parents were in the audience when he turned Hamlet's To be or not to be soliloquy into a total disaster.

I **Euphony**. *Adj*: **euphonious**. From a Greek word meaning 'pleasant-sounding'.

Names into Words

Shrapnel, those lethally jagged lumps of metal that were collected as souvenirs by small boys after bomber raids in the Second World War and that have caused terrible damage to untold numbers of soldiers and civilians, was invented by an English artillery officer in 1784. Henry Shrapnel was only a lieutenant when he developed his idea of packing shot into a cannon ball that would explode in mid-air. The British Army took up his idea, and a series of promotions followed. Shrapnel was a Major General by the time he retired, on the more than comfortable special pension of £1,200 a year.

The Moving Finger Writes

A   A manuscript in which the original text has been imperfectly obliterated and written over by new text.

B   The right-hand page of a book.

C   The left-hand page of a book.

D   Ancient Egyptian picture writing.

E   Wedge-shaped marks on clay tablets, impressed to keep records in Assyria and other ancient civilisations.

F   The largest regular size of a book or page; a printer's sheet, folded once to make two leaves, each c. 38 cm (15 in.) in height. Also the page number in a book.

G   A printer's sheet folded twice, to make four leaves and a page measuring 22.9 cm by 15.2 cm (9 in. by 6 in.).

H   A printer's sheet folded three times, to make eight leaves and a page measuring 25.6 cm by 20.3 cm (10 in. by 8 in.).

Clues

A   10 letters: *p--------t*

B   5 letters: *r----*

C   5 letters: *v----*

D   13 letters: *h-----------s*

E   9 letters: *c--------*

F   5 letters: *f----*

G   6 letters: *qu----*

H   6 letters: *o-----*

See page 10 for answers

Answers, Word Origins and Usage

A **Palimpsest**. Latin *palim* (again) + *psestus* (rubbed smooth).

B **Recto**. Latin for 'right'. Memory-jogger: a rectangle contains four right angles.

C **Verso**. Latin *verso folio* (on the turned leaf).

D **Hieroglyphics**.

E **Cuneiform**. Latin *cuneus* (wedge).

F **Folio**. Latin *folium* (leaf).

G **Quarto**. Latin for 'one-fourth'. Memory-jogger: a sheet of paper is folded to make four leaves, each one quarter the size of the original sheet.

H **Octavo**. Latin *octo* (eight). Memory-jogger: a sheet of paper is folded to make eight leaves.

Names into Words

The political analyst Niccolò Machiavelli (1469–1527) lived in Italy during the Renaissance, when artistic genius rose to new heights and skullduggery sank to new depths. He observed the struggles for power and concluded that those who rose to the top were usually the most single-minded and unscrupulous. His book *The Prince*, published in 1532, draws lessons from the life of Cesare Borgia, son of Pope Alexander VI. Cesare found ways to put enemies and rivals out of the way – most of them permanently. Machiavelli draws the moral that public life and private life are to be judged by different standards and that the end justifies the means. Rightly or wrongly, his analysis has been taken as his advice. To accuse somebody of **Machiavellian** behaviour is to imply an unscrupulous approach to life and the use of deceit to get ahead.

The Moving Finger Writes

A   A symbol representing an object or idea but, as for example in Chinese, giving no guidance on how a word is pronounced.

B   Ancient Germanic alphabet used by Anglo-Saxons and Vikings.

C   Ancient Egyptian symbol, usually enclosed in an oval or a rectangle, giving the name or recording the virtues of a pharaoh or god.

D   A book made up of manuscripts.

E   Descriptive of a book with a high content of obscenity.

F   Writings about the lives of saints or saintly figures.

G   Novel based on the lives of real people, but with names and minor details changed.

H   Writing that follows the flow of a person's thoughts, no matter how disjointed, illogical or fanciful they may be.

Clues

A   8 letters: *id*------

B   5 letters: *r*----

C   9 letters: *car*------

D   5 letters: *c*----

E   12 letters: *sc*----------

F   11 letters: *ha*---------

G   3 words, 5, 1 and 4 letters: *r*---- *à c*---

H   3 words, 6, 2 and 13 letters: *s*------ *o*- *co*------------

See page 12 for answers

Answers, Word Origins and Usage

A **Ideogram**. Greek *idea* (form) + *gram* (something written).

B **Runic**. From an Old Norse word meaning 'magic sign'.

C **Cartouche**. Italian *cartoccia* (paper, card).

D **Codex**. Latin *codex* (board, book of laws).

E **Scatological**. From a Greek word meaning 'dung'.

F **Hagiography**. Greek *hagios* (holy). The *hagiographa* is a group of twelve books in the Hebrew Bible.

G **Roman à clef**. Taken directly from the French.

H **Stream of consciousness**.

As Others See Us... and We See Them

It happens more often than we realize that we foist words associated with coarse behaviour, unsavoury habits and regrettable weaknesses on to other nations. All that can be said in mitigation is that sometimes they return the compliment. We speak of *Dutch Courage, French Leave* and *French Letters* (called 'Capotes Anglaises' by the French). A mild swearword passes our lips and we excuse it with *'Pardon my French!'* There are quite a few expressions too, which are so foreign to the British temperament that we have no word for them and are left having to use the original language: *Schadenfreude, blitzkrieg, coup d'état*.

Divided by a Common Language

American English, after breaking away from its British parent, has developed in a way that can sometimes lead to misunderstandings. A host of words and phrases that originated in the United States are now fully accepted in Britain. *Brownie points, blue chip investments, brunch, buddy* and giving someone the *bum's rush* have all, as it were, applied to take on dual citizenship. To stay with the letter *b*, the term billion, defined in British dictionaries of the last generation as 1,000,000 million, is now universally taken to mean 1,000 million – the meaning it has always carried in the USA.

Figures of Speech

If you need words that will punch above their weight, an easy way to call them up is to fall back on figures of speech. Some have already been mentioned in previous quizzes. Other useful figures of speech are set out below.

A   A comparison or analogy that uses the words as or like – as in: a face as bleak as an Arctic winter.

B   A comparison or analogy which, without using like or as, draws attention to points of similarity – as in: Would you be an angel and post this letter for me?

C   The linking of two words in an incongruous or unexpected way – as in: After putting a tremendous effort into his final appeal to the jury, the defence lawyer rested his case and his leg.

D   Exaggeration for the sake of effect – as in: I'm so hungry I could eat a horse.

E   Repetition of initial sounds of words in a phrase or sentence – as in Spiro Agnew's 'nattering nabobs of negativism'.

F   The use of a single word to convey the meaning of an entire phrase – as when saying or writing, '1,000 head' to represent 1,000 head of cattle.

G   Understatement by which what might be taken as a negative judgement is plainly understood to be a positive one – as in: That was no small sacrifice you made, giving away your Cup Final ticket.

H A form of wit or attempted wit in which words are clearly understood to convey the opposite of their literal meanings – as in: Don't you agree that if you are going to give up giving up smoking for the twentieth time it would be a good idea for all of us to start breaking a few New Year resolutions?

I A mocking, contemptuous style of attempted wit – as in: Of course we all know that when things go wrong it's never your fault.

J A switch-around of words in two parallel phrases to make a point. Example: You can take the boy out of Liverpool, but you can't take Liverpool out of the boy.

Clues

A   6 letters: *s-----*

B   8 letters: *m-------*

C   6 letters: *zeu---*

D   9 letters: *hy-------*

E   12 letters: *all---------*

F   10 letters: *syn-------*

G   7 letters: *lit----*

H   5 letters: *ir---*

I   7 letters: *s------*

J   8 letters: *chi-----*

See page 16 for answers

Answers, Word Origins and Usage

A   **Simile**. Memory-jogger: similar.

B   **Metaphor**. *Adv*: **metaphorically**. From the Greek *metaphora* (transfer).

C   **Zeugma**. Latin *zeugma* (uniting).

D   **Hyperbole**. Latin *hyperbole* (to an excessive degree).

E   **Alliteration**. *Adj*: **alliterative**. Latin *ad* (to) + *litera* (letter).

F   **Synecdoche**. From a Greek word meaning 'take up'. *Pron*: **sinekdakee**.

G   **Litotes**. Greek *litos* (plain, meagre). *Pron*: **lietoeteez**.

H   **Irony**. *Adj*: **ironical**. From a Greek word meaning 'simulated ignorance'.

I   **Sarcasm**. Latin *sarcasmus* (to tear flesh).

J   **Chiasmus**. Greek *khiasmos* (crosswise).

Journey to the Centre the of the Earth

A Earth's solid outer layer, reaching from the crust to about 75 km (46.6 miles) deep.

B An abandoned project that was meant to drill an exploratory hole through the ocean bed.

C Semi-fluid layer of molten rock on which the continents and the ocean floors are adrift.

D Solid part of the Earth's mantle, lying above the fluid outer core. It begins at a depth of c. 250 km (155 miles) and reaches down to c. 2,900 km (1,800 miles).

E Study of the way in which the continents and ocean floors float on a 'sea' of molten rock.

F Earth's landmass some 200 million years ago, when all the continents were joined together.

G The two super-continents that existed some 180 million years ago.

H Region in which, under enormous pressures, one section of a continental plate is forced beneath another.

I Body of porous water-bearing rock beneath the ground.

J The type of well drilled to reach trapped water, which rises to the surface under hydrostatic pressure.

Clues

A 11 letters: *l---------e*

B 6 letters: *mo----*

C 13 letters: *asth---------*

D 10 letters: *mes-------*

E 2 words, 5 letters and 9: *pl--- te-------*

F 6 letters: *pan---*

G 2 words, 8 letters and 12: *La------ and Gon---------*

H 2 words, 10 letters and 4: *sub------- z---*

I 7 letters: *aq-----*

J 8 letters: *ar------*

See page 18 for answers

17

Answers, Word Origins and Usage

A **Lithosphere**. Greek *lithort* (stone).

B **Mohole**. The **moho** is the boundary between the Earth's crust and its mantle.

C **Asthenosphere**. Greek *asthenes* (weak).

D **Mesosphere**. Greek *mesos* (middle).

E **Plate tectonics**. Greek *tekton* (builder).

F **Pangaea**. Greek *pan* (all).

G **Laurasia** and **Gondwanaland**.

H **Subduction zone**.

I **Aquifer**. Latin *aqua* (water). Memory-jogger: aquarium.

J **Artesian**. From Artois, France, where the first wells of this type were drilled.

Divided by a Common Language

In Britain, a **poll tax** is payable by every adult in the land, with its name based on an old meaning of the word poll: the top of the head. It comes as no surprise that it was never a wildly popular way of raising cash for the government. The last time the tax was tried, even though given the less provocative name of Council Tax, the reaction to it played an important part in the downfall of Margaret Thatcher.

In America, a poll tax was a tax applied in the past by several States, which people had to pay to secure the right to vote – that is, to go to the polls on Election Day. Again, it is unlikely to have raised wild enthusiasm. In Australia, by contrast, with both Britain and the USA, it is illegal for those qualified to vote not to exercise their right, and they face a fine.

Fears and Phobias

The Greeks had a word for irrational fears and intense hatreds, and it has come down to us in its original form. The complexity of modern society means that we have all the phobias known to the Ancient Greeks, and quite a few more. How many of the following can you put a name to?

A   Exaggerated fear of open spaces.
B   Fear of confined spaces.
C   Abnormal fear of the dark.
D   Irrational fear of spiders.
E   Fear of the number thirteen.
F   Dislike of foreigners and other nations.
G   Fear of dogs.
H   Fear of cats.
I   Fear of horses.
J   Abnormal fear of rats and mice.

Clues

A   11 letters: *ago--------*
B   14 letters: *c-------------*
C   11 letters: *sco--------*
D   13 letters: *ara----------*
E   17 letters: *tri--------------*
F   10 letters: *xen-------*
G   10 letters: *cy--------*
H   10 letters: *ga--------*
I   11 letters: *hip--------*
J   10 letters: *mus-------*

See page 20 for answers

Answers, Word Origins and Usage

A **Agoraphobia**. In the cities of Ancient Greece the *agora* was not only a bustling marketplace; it was also the place for public meetings, with rousing speeches, denunciations and noisy cheering. Small wonder that those who were paranoid about intrusions on their privacy kept well away.

B **Claustrophobia**. *Adj*: **claustrophobic**.

C **Scotophobia**. *Adj*: **scotophobic**. Greek *skotos* (darkness).

D **Arachnophobia**. Greek *arachne* (spider). All eight-legged insect-like creatures belong to the family *arachnidae*.

E **Triskaidekaphobia**. Greek *kai* (three) + *deka* (ten).

F **Xenophobia**. *Adj*: **xenophobic**. Greek *xenos* (strange).

G **Cynophobia**. *Adj*: **cynophobic**. Greek *kunos* (dog).

H **Gatophobia**. *Adj*: **gatophobic**. Spanish *gato* (cat).

I **Hippophobia**. *Adj*: **hippophobic**. Greek *hippos* (horse). Memory-jogger: Greek chariot races were staged in a hippodrome, a name that was later adopted by many places of entertainment, notably cinemas, in Britain.

J **Musophobia**. Latin *mus* (mouse). Both rats and mice belong to the *muridae* family.

Behind the Word

The dictionary definition of **serendipity** is that it is a happy discovery, made by chance. The word itself, however, is a happy invention, made deliberately. It was coined in 1794 by the essayist and poet Horace Walpole, after reading a fairy tale. *The Three Princes of Serendip* (an old name for Sri Lanka) told of three noblemen who were always discovering things they had not been searching for – and always with a fortunate outcome.

Fears and Phobias

A Fear of butterflies and moths.

B Fear of water and of swallowing.

C Dread of heights.

D Fear of being buried alive.

E Fear of being poisoned.

F Fear of catching an infectious disease

G Intense dislike of the entire male sex.

H Dread of stuttering or public speaking.

I Fear of snakes.

J Abnormal fear of speed.

Clues

A 11 letters: *pte*--------

B 11 letters: *hyd*--------

C 10 letters: *ac*--------

D 11 letters: *tap*--------

E 12 letters: *tox*---------

F 14 letters: *mic*-----------

G 11 letters: *and*--------

H Two choices, 10 letters and 12: *lal*------- and *glo*---------

I 13 letters: *oph*----------

J 10 letters: *tac*-------

See page 22 for answers

Answers, Word Origins and Usage

A **Pterophobia**. Greek *pteron* (wing). Memory-jogger: pterodactyl, a long-extinct flying dinosaur.

B **Hydrophobia**. *Adj*: **hydrophobic**. Memory-joggers: hydroelectric, hydrant.

C **Acrophobia**. Greek *akron* (peak).

D **Taphophobia**. Greek *taphos* (tomb, grave).

E **Toxicophobia**. Greek *toxikon* (poison).

F **Microbiophobia**. Greek *mikros* (small – as in microbe).

G **Androphobia**. Greek *anthropos* (man). Memory-jogger: philanthropist.

H **Lalophobia** and **glossophobia**. Greek *lalein* (to speak) and *glossa* (tongue).

I **Ophidiophobia**. Greek *ophis,* which relates to snakes.

J **Tacophobia**. Greek *takhos* (speed). Memory-jogger: the tachometer that measures and displays the speed of a car.

Names into Words

Joseph Stalin, so ruthless that he was nicknamed (though never to his face) the Red Tsar, was convinced that, whatever the cost, the industrial might of the USSR had to catch up with that of the West. In a series of five-year plans he pushed Soviet output far beyond what seemed reasonable limits. Astonishingly, some Soviet workers made his ambitions look modest. In the Donbass mining region normal output was a hefty six-and-a-half tons of coal per man per five-hour shift. On 30 August 1935, the Donbass miner Alexander Stakhanov hacked out 104 tons during an all-night shift. This earned him adulation, a sevenfold pay rise and a place in the world's encyclopaedias and dictionaries. **Stakhanovite** came into use to describe zealous workers in any field whose output set new standards.

Brush Up Your Latin

A   Pushing an argument or pursuing an activity to an excessive degree – so much so that it becomes disgusting to other people.

B   A title or position that has no payment attached, but is granted purely as an honour.

C   Signed on behalf of somebody else.

D   Taken outdoors, enjoying the fresh air.

E   Among other things…

F   Demonstrating that a line of reasoning is false by pushing it to logical conclusions which are clearly and self-evidently absurd.

G   Before the war, particularly the American Civil War.

H   Caught in some nefarious act.

I   Term applied to somebody regarded as the first among equals.

J   'It is a sweet and fitting thing.' (The Roman poet Horace.)

Clues

A   2 words, 2 letters and 7: *a- n------*

B   2 words, 7 letters and 5: *h------ c----*

C   2 words, both with 3 letters: *p-- p--*

D   2 words, 2 letters and 6: *a- f-----*

E   2 words, 5 letters and 4: *i---- a---*

F   3 words, 8, 2 and 8 letters: *r------- a- a-------*

G   2 words, 4 letters and 6: *a--- b-----*

H   2 words, 9 letters and 7: *fl------- d------*

I   3 words, 6, 5 and 5 letters: *p----- i---- p----*

J   3 words, 5, 2 and 7 letters: *d---- e- d------*

See page 24 for answers

Answers, Word Origins and Usage

A **Ad nauseam**. Example: You have hammered home your point *ad nauseam*, so please give it a rest.

B **Honoris causa**. Example: Jane had no formal qualifications but was given a seat on the board *honoris causa*, because of her charity work.

C **Per pro**. Example: My boss is so lazy he expects me to sign all of his letters *per pro*.

D **Al fresco**. Example: The garden is especially lovely today, so let's eat *al fresco*.

E **Inter alia**. Example: Dare I suggest, *inter alia*, that since next door was burgled last night there are better places to hide the key than under the doormat?

F **Reductio ad absurdum**. If a speaker were to claim that every worker in the land was paid above the average wage he would be demolishing his own argument with a *reductio ad absurdum*.

G **Ante bellum**. When the war in question is America's Civil War, the two words become one: The surviving *antebellum* mansions have the grace of an era in architecture that will never return.

H **Flagrante delicto**. Example: The suspect was photographed slipping Mr Beckford's wallet into his own pocket – a clear case of *flagrante delicto*.

I **Primus inter pares**. Example: It rapidly became obvious that although the gang had no official leader, Pedro was *primus inter pares*.

J **Dulce et decorum**. The full line, from the Roman poet Horace, is *Dulce et decorum est pro patria mori*. (It is a sweet and fitting thing to die for one's country.)

Divided by a Common Language

No matter how many American words have, as it were, taken on dual nationality there are many others that stay firmly in the land of their birth. Here are some: *bleachers* (cheap, uncovered seats in a sports stadium), *pinch-hitter* (a substitute batter in baseball, and hence a substitute in any job), *potato chips* (crisps), *corn* (maize), *cotton candy* (candyfloss), *crawfish* (crayfish), *jelly* (jam), *jello* (jelly), *car* (railway carriage).

Brush Up Your Latin

A Genuine, in good faith, with every intention of performing what is promised.

B A way of performing a task that follows a pattern and is typical of a person.

C Hail and farewell!

D The 'divide and rule' technique of weakening enemies and keeping subject nations under control.

E A form of reasoning that starts by establishing the cause then, by deduction, arrives at the effect.

F A form of reasoning that starts with the effect and from that induces what must be the cause.

G A conclusion that is intended to follow logically and inevitably from what has just been stated, but in fact does not.

H Something that must be accepted as a fact, whether it is rightful and supported by law or not.

I Something regarded as right because it is supported by law or by long-standing custom.

J The voice of the people.

Clues

A 2 words, each with 4 letters: *b--- f---*

B 2 words, 5 letters and 8: *m---- o-------*

C 3 words, 3, 5 and 4 letters: *a-- a---- v---*

D 3 words, 6, 2 and 6 letters: *d----- e- i-----*

E 2 words, 1 letter and 6: *a p-----*

F 2 words, 1 letter and 10: *a p----------*

G 2 words, 3 letters and 8: *n-- s-------*

H 2 words, 2 letters and 5: *d- f----*

I 2 words, 2 letters and 4: *d- j---*

J 2 words, 3 letters and 6: *v-- p-----*

See page 26 for answers

Answers, Word Origins and Usage

A **Bona fide**. Example: I wouldn't put my trust in that man if I were you. He isn't exactly *bona fide*.

B **Modus operandi** (a manner of working). Sherlock Holmes's *modus operandi*, when faced with a particularly baffling case, was to begin by excluding the impossible. He believed that whatever remained, however improbable, was the truth.

C **Ave atque vale!** A greeting and a goodbye, all in one.

D **Divide et impera**. Divide and rule – as the Romans did in Gaul and the British in India.

E **A priori**. An example of *a priori* reasoning is the theory that Hitler plunged the world into war because his paintings were rejected by the art school in Vienna.

F **A posteriori**. An example of *a posteriori* reasoning could be the widely held conviction that burning fossil fuels has made a major contribution to global warming.

G **Non sequitur** (It does not follow). Example: It's a plain *non sequitur* for you to say that since my eight-year-old daughter adores Vivaldi she will never be able to find any pleasure in soul music.

H **De facto** (in fact).

I **De jure** (by right). Stalin's *de jure* title was General Secretary of the Communist Party, which does not sound tremendously impressive; but he was beyond challenge as the Soviet Union's *de facto* ruler.

J **Vox populi**. The full phrase, from a letter by the English theologian Alcuin (*c.* 735–804) to the emperor Charlemagne, is *vox populi, vox dei* (the voice of the people is the voice of God). The abbreviation *vox pop* is commonly used nowadays by television, radio and newspaper journalists when, seeking to gauge public opinion, they interview a random selection of people.

Brush Up Your Latin

A   The situation as it stands; the way things are arranged at present.

B   All relevant, other things being equal.

C   Legal and moral position of anybody who stands in as the parent or parents of a child.

D   To speak or perform without rehearsal or any other preparation.

E   A course of action that is beyond a person's legal authority or power to perform.

F   Make the best use of what you have, and live for today, rather than worry about tomorrow.

G   A lot, packed into a little.

H   Art is long, and time is fleeting.

Clues

A   2 words, 6 letters and 3: *s----- q--*

B   2 words, 7 letters each: *c------ p------*

C   3 words, 2, 4 and 8 letters: *i- l--- p-------*

D   2 words, 2 letters and 3: *a- l--*

E   2 words, 5 letters each: *u---- v----*

F   2 words, 5 letters and 4: *c---- d---*

G   3 words, 6, 2 and 5 letters: *m----- i- p----*

H   4 words: 3, 5, 4 and 6 letters: *a-- l---- v--- b-----*

See page 28 for answers

Answers, Word Origins and Usage

A **Status quo**: Before we get tangled up in minor details over these new proposals, let's just remind ourselves of the *status quo*. The Latin tag for 'the way things were' is *status quo ante*.

B **Ceteris paribus**: If the builder wants payment in advance and has a good reputation then, *ceteris paribus*, we should stump up.

C **In loco parentis**: When Johnny was pushed over after being taunted by playground bullies and twisted his ankle, his teacher was *in loco parentis* and should have intervened.

D **Ad lib**. A clever comedian can always score by putting down a heckler with a witty *ad lib*.

E **Ultra vires**: In saying that Jones was obviously guilty before hearing a word of his defence, the judge was clearly acting *ultra vires*.

F **Carpe diem**. The phrase can also be taken as an encouragement to seize the day by taking advantage of any opportunities that present themselves.

G **Multum in parvo**: This new flyweight may look skinny and undernourished but once in the ring he is *multum in parvo*.

H **Ars longa, vita brevis**. Literally, 'Art is long, life is short.'

Behind the Word

It is regarded as an insult nowadays, and far from politically correct, to describe anybody as a **cretin**, but when the word was first bestowed upon people who were handicapped both physically and mentally it was intended as an act of kindness. Lack of iodine in the soil of areas in the Swiss Alps often damaged the development of the thyroid glands in families who lived there. Travellers and some of those local people who did not have the resulting symptoms shunned those who did.

They had to be reminded that the sufferers, however they looked, were still Christians and should be treated as such. And in those parts the word for Christian was Crétin.

Brush Up Your Latin

A   An arrangement made for a specific purpose and discarded once it is achieved.

B   It is the buyer's responsibility to check before buying that the goods are sound and fit for purpose.

C   There are as many opinions as there are men to give them.

D   A term often applied jokingly to a place such as a study or even a garden shed, where complete privacy is sought and found.

E   This is how the glory of the world ends.

F   A book or some other cherished item that is constantly carried by its owner and often consulted.

G   An exceptional, rarely encountered, person or object.

H   An essential condition, without which no agreement can be reached.

I   A favour to be returned, on the principle of 'You scratch my back and I'll scratch yours.'

J   Perfection, a role model, attainment or standard that cannot be surpassed.

Clues

A   2 words, 2 letters and 3: *a- h--*

B   2 words, both 6 letters: *c----- e-----*

C   4 words, 4, 7, 3 and 10 letters: *q--- h------ t-- s----------*

D   2 words, 7 letters and 9: *s------ s--------*

E   4 words, 3, 7, 6 and 5 letters: *s-- t------ g----- m----*

F   2 words, 4 letters and 5: *v--- m----*

G   2 words, both 4 letters: *r--- a---*

H   3 words, 4, 3 and 3 letters: *s--- q-- n--*

I   3 words, 4, 3 and 3 letters: *q--- p-- q--*

J   3 words, 2, 4 and 5 letters: *n- p--- u----*

See page 30 for answers

Answers, Word Origins and Usage

A **Ad hoc** (towards this). Example: The cricket club is setting up an *ad hoc* inquiry to decide whether their demon bowler is bowling or throwing.

B **Caveat emptor!** (Let the buyer beware!). Example: It's too late now to make a fuss. You should have remembered *caveat emptor* and kept the money in your pocket.

C **Quot homines, tot sententiae**. The saying may be abbreviated, as in: The candidate soon realised that the more people he questioned the more it was going to be a case of *quot homeines*.

D **Sanctum sanctorum** (the holy of holies). Example: Fred can't be disturbed just now. He's in his *sanctum sanctorum*, discussing the problem of moss on the lawn with his mowing machine.

E **Sic transit Gloria mundi**. These words are more likely to be uttered when some grand enterprise collapses and comes to a close, rather than taken literally and spoken when everything worthwhile ends.

F **Vade mecum** (Go with me). Example: Samuel never went anywhere without Defoe's *Robinson Crusoe*, his *vade mecum*.

G **Rara avis** (a rare bird). Example: A 5 ft 5 in. star is indeed a *rara avis* in modern basketball.

H **Sine qua non** (without which, not). Example: It is a *sine qua non* that I will not buy the house unless you get your neighbours' written agreement that they will never again grow a leylandii hedge.

I **Quid pro quo** (something for something). Example: The Lloyds gave a fortnight's stay in their Lake District cottage to an American family as a *quid pro quo* for their stay in Florida.

J **Ne plus ultra** (no further beyond). This prohibition was said to be engraved on the Pillars of Hercules at the Straits of Gibraltar as a warning to captains and crews not to risk the perils awaiting them in the Atlantic.

Quote or Misquote?

A It is a far better thing that I do now than I have ever done before
   – Sydney Carton, in Charles Dickens's *A Tale of Two Cities*

B It is never difficult to distinguish between a Scotsman with a
   grievance and a ray of sunshine – P. G. Wodehouse (1881–1975)

C Rivers of blood – Enoch Powell (1912–98)

D Elementary, my dear Watson – Sherlock Holmes

E Men never make passes at girls who wear glasses – Dorothy
   Parker (1893–1967)

See page 32 for answers

Quotations check

A Misquote. What Sydney Carton said when he sacrificed his life for the woman he loved was: 'It is a far, far better thing that I do, than I have ever done.'

B Correct quote.

C Misquote. Enoch Powell did not use these words in his 1968 Birmingham speech on the subject of unrestricted immigration, though they give a fair summary of his views. He said: 'As I look ahead I am filled with foreboding. Like the Roman, I seem to see the River Tiber foaming with much blood.'

D Misquote. Nowhere in Conan Doyle's stories of the great detective does Holmes use this phrase.

E Misquote, but a near miss. Switch 'never' to 'seldom'.

Divided by a Common Language

A Briton with a grievance will **protest** against it, while an American will simply *protest* it: Members of the gun lobby strongly *protested* any attempt to curb the use of assault weapons. Sometimes, however, a word that grates on British ears turns out to be of solid British parentage. One such is *gotten*, used as the past tense of got. The writer John Aubrey (1626–97) uses gotten quite freely in his *Brief Lives*. And Aubrey was a founder member of the Royal Society, so his authority is not to be lightly challenged.

Politics and Government

A   A parliament or similar body in which law-making powers are shared by two chambers, as in the US Congress, with its Senate and House of Representatives.

B   Self-governing, independent.

C   The redrawing of the boundaries of a constituency to gain an unfair electoral advantage for one's own party.

D   Political term for the working class.

E   Somebody regarded as of low birth and modest cultural aspiration.

F   A group of trained and committed activists within a revolutionary political party.

G   A rule that has become law because it was enacted by the appropriate authority.

H   Influential group within a political party that selects the candidates and decides policy.

I   Restructuring of how a country is governed, so people are treated more fairly.

J   Increased readiness by a government to explain and justify its activities to the people.

Clues

A   2 words, 9 letters and 11: *b*-------- *l*----------

B   10 letters: *a*--------

C   11 letters: *ge*---------

D   11 letters: *p*----------

E   8 letters: *pl*------

F   5 letters: *c*----

G   7 letters: *s*------

H   6 letters: *c*-----

I   11 letters: *per*--------

J   8 letters: *g*-------

See page 34 for answers

Answers, Word Origins and Usage

A **Bicameral legislature**. Latin *bi* (two) + *camera* (chamber) and *legis* (law) + *latio* (proposing).

B **Autonomous**. *Noun*: **autonomy**. Greek *autos* (self) + *nomos* (law), hence 'ruled by its own laws'.

C **Gerrymander**. In 1812, Elbridge Gerry, governor of Massachusetts, manipulated electoral boundaries to give Republicans a majority in the state senate. The shape of the new boundaries on a map was so complicated that commentators compared it to the outline of a salamander.

D **Proletariat**. Latin *proletarius* (those whose contribution to the state was made not with money or property but with offspring, in the production of which they were assumed to be prolific). The word is sometimes shortened to *proles*. Marxists refer to *proletarians* who have little or no interest in revolutionary politics as the *lumpenproletariat*.

E **Plebeian**. In Ancient Rome the common people were known as *plebs*. They had their own assembly and voted in it by *plebiscite*.

F **Cadre**. Latin *quadrus* (square).

G **Statute**. *Adj*: **statutory**. Latin *statuere* (to decree, establish).

H **Caucus**. Origin uncertain, but the term was first used in the USA and may come from the Algonquin word *caucauasu*.

I **Perestroika**. Russian: restructuring of a country's economic and political systems.

J **Glasnost**. Russian: Great openness about the government's activities and policies.

Signs of the Times

The Anglo-Saxons Arrive

The departure of the Roman legions was an open invitation to Germanic-speaking Angles, Saxons and Jutes to step up their raids on the shores of what was to become England. And those who came as raiders began increasingly to stay as settlers. By the end of the seventh century, with the Celts pushed out to Wales and Scotland, there were seven Anglo-Saxon kingdoms in England.

From what is termed Old English by modern scholars we have inherited a vocabulary for the basic things in life, from family relationships to food. Father, mother, sister and brother all have their roots in Old English. The word loaf began as *hlaf* and the word for the man providing it, the *hlaf-weard*, gave us the word 'lord'. He and his *huswif* would have to walk many a *furlangh* through the countryside, so *werfotadl* (foot pain, now known as gout) was highly unwelcome. Their names for the creatures that played a part in their lives have given us such words as wolf, ox, goat, pig and mouse.

Anglo-Saxon place names include: *-ing* (the people of), *-ham* (village, homestead), *-tun* (farmstead), *-stow* (a meeting place), *- ingham* (people of the homestead), *-bury* (a fortified place), *ley* and *lea* (a clearing in woodland) and *ford*. The settlers found a name for their new country: *Englaland*. Go forward a millennium and almost the same word is chanted by fans on the football terraces: EN-GER-LAND!

Signs of the Times

Invasion of the Vikings

In AD 793, a band of Vikings landed on the Northumbrian coast near Lindisfarne, a monastery housing the relics of the most revered man in England, the Venerable Bede. They slaughtered monks, seized church treasures and set a pattern of terror that was to be repeated in places where plunder was to be had. What began for these wild marauders from the *viks* (creeks) of Scandinavia as sporadic raiding and easy pickings developed over the next 200 years into full-scale invasion and settlement. The Vikings, many of them Danes, came to rule over much of Northern and Eastern England – a region known as the Danelaw.

Wherever they put down roots they left a legacy of new words. Place names ending *-by, -thorpe, -dale, -beck, -thwaite* and *-toft* point to a Scandinavian origin. So does the ending *-son* in such names as Jackson and Johnson. Among the words they introduced are birth, dirt, knife, scare, rotten, ugly and thrift. Many a stream or brook in the North East is known as a beck, from the Old Norse *bekk*; and many a hill is a fell, from Old Norse *fiall*, a mountain. Another Danish legacy, in a period when hygiene and personal freshness were not of primary concern, was the word *loppe* (lop) – known to the rest of itching, scratching England as a flea.

Politics and Government

A Government by the rich.

B Government by the few.

C Government by religious leaders.

D To discontinue a parliamentary session without dissolving the Parliament.

E To seek to persuade voters to change their allegiance.

F The power given by Parliament to a government minister to make laws, rules and regulations.

G A Crown office that no longer exists, but is applied for by MPs who wish to resign from Parliament.

H Edited for publication, with sensitive information obliterated.

I A notice by an MP of a motion for a House of Commons debate that will not take place.

J A high-ranking civil servant who has become a master manipulator of words.

Clues

A 10 letters: *pl*--------

B 9 letters: *ol*-------

C 9 letters: *th*-------

D 8 letters: *pro*-----

E 11 letters: *pro*--------

F 2 words, 9 letters and 11: *d*-------- *l*----------

G 2 words, 8 letters and 9: *C*------- *H*-------

H 8 letters: *r*-------

I 3 words, 5, 3 and 6 letters: *E*---- *D*-- *M*-----

J 8 letters: *m*-------

See page 38 for answers

Answers, Word Origins and Usage

A **Plutocracy**. Greek *ploutos* (wealth). A member of such a ruling group is a plutocrat.

B **Oligarchy**. Greek *oligos* (few, little). A member of such a group, in which control is often passed down within families, as in North Korea, is an oligarch – a term that is also applied to super-rich Russian business-men, because they operate in an *oligopoly* (a section of the business world in which competitors are markedly rare).

C **Theocracy**. Greek *theos* (god). A member of such a group is a theocrat. Memory-jogger: theology.

D **Prorogue**. Latin *prorogare* (to prolong): The Crown has a constitution-al right to call, dismiss or prorogue Parliament.

E **Proselytise**. *Pron*: **proselytise**. Latin *proselytus* (stranger, convert). The term can also apply in the field of religion – indeed, to a conversion of any kind.

F **Delegated legislation**.

G **Chiltern Hundreds** – a non-existent but at times highly convenient address.

H **Redacted**. Latin *redigere* (to drive back, revise). The term originally meant simply that information had been edited for publication. It has been used when names and addresses, for example, are obliterated, often for security reasons but in some cases to avoid embarrassment to senior business people or celebrities.

I **Early Day Motion**. MPs use the device to show that the topic is impor-tant and to get some idea of what support they might expect if it should become 'live' in the future.

J **Mandarin**. Taken directly from the name for a member of the highest grade of civil servants in imperial China.

Quote or Misquote?

A   The Assyrian came down like the wolf on the fold – *The Bible*

B   I speak Spanish to God, Italian to women, French to men and German to my horse – Holy Roman Emperor Charles V (1500–58)

C   Play it again, Sam – Humphrey Bogart, in *Casablanca*

D   I expect you'll be becoming a schoolmaster, sir. That's what most of the gentlemen does, sir, that gets sent down for indecency – Evelyn Waugh, in *Decline and Fall*

E   Tomorrow to fresh fields and pastures new – John Milton, in *Lycidas*

F   Alas, poor Yorick! I knew him well – Shakespeare's *Hamlet*

See page 40 for answers

Quotations check

A The quotation is correct but the attribution is wrong. The line is from Lord Byron's poem *The Destruction of Sennacherib*.

B Correct – or at least the quotation has been attributed to Charles and to nobody else.

C Incorrect. What bar owner Rick, played by Humphrey Bogart, said was: '*Play it, Sam. Play* As Time Goes By.'

D Correct quotation.

E Incorrect. What Milton wrote was '*Tomorrow to fresh woods…*' After all, fields and pastures are much the same thing and Milton was not likely to be guilty of tautology.

F Incorrect. The line should be: '*Alas, poor Yorick! I knew him, Horatio.*'

Politics and Government

A   A government-issued report containing information on a topic to be debated in the House of Commons.

B   A means of limiting the time spent debating a bill in Parliament, used when a government wants to rush a proposal through.

C   A ministerial order that does not need the authority of a parliamentary vote.

D   A particularly zealous and energetic member of the Communist Party.

E   The dominance of one state over another.

F   The study of elections, usually motivated by a desire to forecast or shape results.

G   A system working towards bringing a nation's government and main industries under the control of trade unions.

H   An attempt, usually unsuccessful, to buy off aggressive nations by conceding some of their demands.

Clues

A   2 words, each 5 letters: *w---- p----*

B   10 letters: *g---------*

C   3 words, 5, 2 and 7 letters: *O---- i- C------*

D   11 letters: *app--------*

E   8 letters: *heg-----*

F   10 letters: *pse-------*

G   11 letters: *syn--------*

H   11 letters: *app--------*

See page 42 for answers

Answers, Word Origins and Usage

A **White paper**.

B **Guillotine**. Named after the device that brought many lives to a swift conclusion during the French Revolution.

C **Order in Council**. The Council is the Privy Council, originally set up to advise Norman kings but now chiefly confined to a formal role.

D **Apparatchik**. The word is sometimes extended, with humorous intent, to apply to anybody who devotes excessive energy and enthusiasm to a bureaucratic job.

E **Hegemony**. The *g* is soft, as in general.

F **Psephology**. Greek *psephos* (pebble). In ancient Greece, votes were cast by throwing pebbles into a pot – one pot for 'Yes', another for 'No'.

G **Syndicalism**. Greek *sundikos* (together for justice).

H **Appeasement**.

Proverbs in Parallel

All over the world, folk wisdom is encapsulated in proverbs. What is remarkable is how often the proverbs from different nations agree about what matters in life and what is the wisest way to live it.

British: A bird in the hand is worth two in the bush.
German: A sparrow in the hand is better than a pigeon on the roof.

British: A bad workman blames his tools.
French: To a bad workman there is no such thing as a good tool.

British: When in Rome, do as the Romans do.
Spanish: Wherever you go, do what you see.

British: There's one law for the rich, another for the poor.
Russian: The thief who steals three kopeks is hanged. The thief who steals fifty is honoured.

Business and Finance

A   A process intended to pump money into a flagging economy. A nation's central bank electronically buys assets such as bonds from commercial banks, which are then encouraged to lend the newly created money to businesses.

B   Economic demand for a product that is likely to fade fairly rapidly if the price rises.

C   Economic demand that resists falling away as the price of a product or service rises.

D   The theory that governments should not interfere in the workings of the free market.

E   The theory that a nation's wealth is measured by the amount of gold and silver in its coffers, so it should always pursue a favourable balance of trade with other countries.

F   An economic law stating that after initial and urgent needs for goods or services have been met, the satisfaction they bring falls away.

G   The law stating that bad money drives out good.

H   Interest on a loan or investment that increases year by year because interest is paid on the previous year's interest.

I   A voucher or bond acknowledging a debt, backed only by the reputation of the issuer and paying a fixed rate of interest.

Clues

A   2 words, 12 letters and 6: *q----------- e-----*

B   2 words, 7 letters and 6: *e------ d-----*

C   2 words, 9 letters and 6: *i-------- d-----*

D   2 hyphenated words, 7 letters and 5: *l------ f----*

E   12 letters, *mer---------*

F   4 words, 3, 2, 11 and 7 letters: *l-- o- d---------- r------*

G   2 words, 8 letters and 3: *G------'- L--*

H   2 words. 10, 8 letters: *c--------- in------*

I   9 letters: *de-------*

See page 44 for answers

Answers, Word Origins and Usage

A **Quantitative easing**. This remedy leads to inflation, which is considered the lesser of two evils if the newly created money kick-starts a country's prosperity.

B **Elastic demand**. Example: Sea cruises, which go up and down in price according to the weather, the time of year and the general state of the economy.

C **Inelastic demand**. Example: Public school fees, which usually increase every year but always seem able to find willing buyers.

D **Laissez-faire**. French for Let people do what they want to do.

E **Mercantilism**. Italian *mercante* (merchant).

F **Law of diminishing returns**. Example: Robinson Crusoe might plant twenty rows of potatoes on his island but finding them sufficient for survival would choose some other crop rather than continue with potatoes in the twenty-first row. This law is also applicable to human activities that lie outside the realm of economics.

G **Gresham's Law**. Sir Thomas Gresham (1519–79), a founder member of the Royal Society, used his financial acumen to pay off his country's debts, to build a fortune for himself and to found a college and eight almshouses.

H **Cumulative interest**. Memory-jogger: the interest accumulates.

I **Debenture**. Latin *debenture* (they are owed). Buying a debenture is also a way of securing seats for a number of years at sports and cultural venues.

Names into Words

The Neapolitan banker Lorenzo Tonti (1630–95) had a keen eye for a money-making opportunity. As a young man he moved to France, where he launched a scheme that attracted a number of rich men to pool their money into an annuities fund. As the investors died, one by one, their shares went to the survivors, with the last one to go taking everything that was left. The idea itself lived on, so today we still have the **tontine**.

Business and Finance

A   A careful examination of the financial state and prospects of a firm that is up for sale.

B   Arrangements concerning taxes and other forms of national revenue.

C   Paper money issued by a bank that is not backed by gold in the bank's vaults.

D   A means by which the management can take over a company by borrowing money to acquire a controlling number of shares.

E   Money held as coins, rather than paper.

F   The process of winding up a company which involves calculating its assets and its liabilities.

G   The process, after taking over a failing company, of selling off those parts that remain profitable.

H   The now outmoded theory that in the long run wage levels are set by the minimum amount needed to keep the workforce on a subsistence level.

I   The theory that the best way to tackle inflation and manage a nation's economy is by controlling the amount of money in circulation.

Clues

A   2 words, 3 letters and 9: *d-- dil------*

B   2 words, each 6 letters; *fi---- sy----*

C   9 letters: *fid------*

D   2 words, 9 letters and 6: *l-------- b-----*

E   6 letters: *sp----*

F   11 letters: *l----------*

G   2 words, 5 letters and 9: *a---- s--------*

H   4 words, 4, 3, 2 and 5 letters: *I--- L-- o- W----*

I   10 letters: *mon-------*

See page 46 for answers

Answers, Word Origins and Usage

A **Due diligence**.

B **Fiscal system**. Latin *fiscus* (basket, treasury).

C **Fiduciary**. Latin *fiducia* (trust).

D **Leveraged buyout**, with *lever* pronounced the American way, to rhyme with *ever*, not *leaver*.

E **Specie**.

F **Liquidation**. Latin *liquidare* (to make clear – like a liquid).

G **Asset stripping**.

H **Iron Law of Wages**. The theory was held by a number of influential nineteenth-century economists.

I **Monetarism**. A person who puts the theory into practice is a **monetarist**.

Behind the Word

In Anglo-Saxon England, where the mass of the people worked on the land, the minority who lived in towns were often regarded as oddities. So odd that in some regions they were termed *cockenes* – eggs laid by a cockerel. Londoners, especially, were distrusted and regarded as pampered, even unmanly, when compared with skilled and untiring workers on the land. As the language changed, the *cockenes* became **Cockneys**, with an attitude and a pride of their own.

Over centuries the stigma of being regarded as peculiar began to wither, and to be called a Cockney became a matter of pride – especially after the courage they showed during the Blitz. It was recorded in 1607 that the only people with the right to call themselves Cockneys were those born within the sound of Bow bells – the bells of St Mary-le-Bow, Cheapside.

Earth's Long Journey through the Ages

A   The study of fossils and ancient life.

B   From Earth's creation to *c.* 570 million years ago. A swirling mass of gas cools and a crust is formed, condensing water vapour falls as incessant rain, creating rivers and seas.

C   *c.* 570–500 million years ago. Life, in forms including seaweeds, worms and hard-shelled trilobites, exists only in the sea.

D   *c.* 500–435 million years ago. Primitive fish appear. Life still exists only in the sea.

E   *c.* 435–395 million yeas ago. Plants begin to spread over the land.

F   *c.* 395–345 million years ago. Amphibians crawl out of the seas on to land.

G   *c.* 345–280 million years ago. Coal-forming vegetation accumulates in swamps.

H   *c.* 280–225 million years ago. Reptiles capable of breeding without returning to the sea develop rapidly on land.

I   Ancient mega-continent, made up all of today's continents. It began to break up some 200 million years ago.

J   Two super-continents, formed by the break-up of an ancient mega-continent. They were to break up in their turn, creating today's continents.

Clues

A   13 letters: *pal---------*

B   11 letters, hyphenated: *Pre----------*

C   *8 letters: Cam-----*

D   10 letters: *Ord-------*

E   8 letters: *Sil-----*

F   8 letters: *Dev----*

G   13 letters: *Car----------*

H   7 letters: *Per----*

I   7 letters: *Pan----*

J   8 letters and 12: *Lau------ and Gon---------*

See page 48 for answers

Answers, Word Origins and Usage

A **Palaeontology**. A practitioner: **palaeontologist**. Greek *palai* (long ago).

B **Pre-Cambrian**.

C **Cambrian**. From *Cambria*, the Roman name for Wales, where rocks and fossils of the period were first studied.

D **Ordovician**. From the *Ordovices*, a Celtic tribe of North Wales, where rocks and fossils from this period were first studied.

E **Silurian.** From the *Silures* tribe, who occupied the Welsh region where rocks of the period were first identified.

F **Devonian.** So-named because its rocks and fossils were first identified in Devon.

G **Carboniferous**. Named because widespread deposits of coal were laid down in this period.

H **Permian**. Named after the Russian province of Perm, where rocks of the period were first studied.

I **Pangaea**. Greek *pan* (all) + *gaia* (Earth).

J **Laurasia** and **Gondwanaland**.

Behind the Word

In the days when India was part of the British Empire, the town of Deolali, near Mumbai (then called Bombay), was a staging post for time-served British soldiers who were waiting for a troopship to take them home. Being British, they anglicised the town's name to Doolally and, having done that, they were left with nothing much else to do. Men who had been accustomed to a life packed with drill, orders and duties suddenly found that time was hanging heavily. Some of the less resilient squaddies fell victim to the Doolally Tap – driven out of their minds by a combination of heat, humidity and boredom. The British Empire has long vanished, but the word **doolally** remains in the language as a slightly cheeky way of describing mental disturbance.

Earth's Long Journey through the Ages

A   *c*. 225–190 million years ago. First small dinosaurs on land. Sharks and other large predators dominate the seas.

B   *c*. 190–135 million years ago. Huge plant-eating dinosaurs appear, among them the 30 m (98 ft) brontosaurus. Archaeopteryx, which has claws and feathers, is a forerunner of birds.

C   *c*. 135–65 million years ago. Vast deposits of chalk are laid down, among them the white cliffs of Dover. Dinosaurs dominate on land, sea and in the air.

D   *c*. 65–53 million years ago. Dinosaurs become extinct, allowing mammals to exploit forests and plains.

E   *c*. 53–37 million years ago. Mammals thrive, with ancestral camels, monkeys, rodents, horses and pigs on land and whales in the seas.

F   *c*. 37–26 million years ago. Grasslands spread as forests dwindle. Formation of the Alps begins.

G   *c*. 26–12 million years ago. Sharks more than 18 m (60 ft) long rule the seas. Dog-like carnivores hunt prey on land.

H   *c*. 12–2 million years ago. An epoch of widespread volcanic activity. Some 3.5 million years ago a man-like creature, capable of walking upright, leaves a footprint in Africa.

I   *c*. 2 million–10,000 years ago. Early humans shape tools and live by hunting and gathering. The last Ice Age ends *c*. 10,000 years ago.

J   Began 10,000 years ago. Humans learn to domesticate animals, grow crops and start to live in cities.

K   Any seemingly endless stretch of time; in geology, a billion years.

Clues

A   8 letters: *Tri-----*   G   7 letters: *Mio----*

B   8 letters: *Jur-----*   H   8 letters: *Pli-----*

C   10 letters: *Cre-------*   I   11 letters: *Ple--------*

D   9 letters: *Pal------*   J   8 letters: *Hol-----*

E   6 letters: *Eoc---*   K   4 letters: *a---*

F   9 letters: *Oli------*

See page 50 for answers

Answers, Word Origins and Usage

A **Triassic**. Greek *trias* (three) – referring to a threefold division of rocks in the region of Germany where rocks of the period were first studied.

B **Jurassic**. Named after the Jura Mountains, which straddle the borders of France and Switzerland.

C **Cretaceous**. Latin *creta* (chalk).

D **Paleocene**. Greek *palai* (long ago) + *kainos* (new).

E **Eocene**. Greek *eos* (dawn).

F **Oligocene** Greek *oligos* (few).

G **Miocene**. Greek *meion* (less).

H **Pliocene**. Greek *pleion* (more).

I **Pleistocene**. Greek *pleistos* (most).

J **Holocene**. Greek *holos* (whole).

K **Aeon**. Greek *aion* (age).

Divided by a Common Language

If a prisoner in an American jail is told he will be released **momentarily** it means that in just a few moments the cell gates will open and he will be on his way to freedom. Give the same message to a convict in Britain and he will wonder if there is any point in being allowed out for a brief snatch of time, only to be brought back and hear again the gates slammed behind him. The American momentarily means 'in a moment'; the British momentarily means 'for a moment'.

World Religions

A The belief that the existence of God cannot be known for certain.

B A person, usually young, who assists a priest at the altar.

C A Hindu god who comes to Earth, in human or animal form, at a time of special need.

D A destroyer of statues and other religious images.

E Muhammad's flight from Mecca to Medina in AD 622.

F A proclamation by the Roman Catholic Church that somebody has joined the ranks of the blessed and is considered worthy of promotion to sainthood.

G A declaration by the Roman Catholic Church that somebody led such a holy life that he or she has been made a saint.

H A Roman Catholic who refused to attend Church of England services.

I A person who rejects his or her religious faith.

J A set of beliefs, especially in religious matters, laid down by authority as truths which must be accepted by the faithful.

Clues

A 11 letters: *agn--------*

B 7 letters: *ac-----*

C 6 letters: *av----*

D 10 letters: *ico-------*

E 6 letters: *H-----*

F 13 letters: *bea----------*

G 12 letters: *can---------*

H 8 letters: *rec-----*

I 8 letters: *apo-----*

J 5 letters: *d----*

See page 52 for answers

Answers, Word Origins and Usage

A **Agnosticism**. *Adj and person holding such a belief*: **agnostic**. Greek prefix *a-* (without) + *gnosis* (knowledge).

B **Acolyte**. Greek *akolouthos* (follower).

C **Avatar**. Sanskrit *ava* (down) + *tarati* (he crosses).

D **Iconoclast**. *Adj:* **iconoclastic**. Greek *eikon* (image) + *klan* (to break, smash). The word has extended its territory to apply to somebody who attacks established beliefs in any area of life.

E The **Hegira**. Arabic *hajara* (to depart). Its date marks the start of the Muslim era.

F **Beatification**. *Verb:* **beatify**.

G **Canonisation**.

H **Recusant**. Latin *recusare* (to refuse). The word has extended its original meaning to apply to any dissenter who refuses to accept established authority.

I **Apostate**. Greek *apostasis* (desertion).The word is also applicable to anybody who abandons a principle or a cause that was once accepted.

J **Dogma**. *Adj*: **dogmatic**. Doctrine: *dogmatism*. Greek *dokein* (to think).

Behind the Phrase

Why should handing over money the moment it becomes owed be described as paying 'on the nail'? Even the *Oxford English Dictionary* (OED) has to confess that the source of the phrase is obscure. Up to a generation or so ago it was widely believed that there was a connection between the phrase and four brass pillars standing outside the Corn Exchange at Bristol. Samples of grain would be spread on top of the pillars and if a buyer was satisfied with their quality he would pay 'on the nail'. A nice story, but the OED dismisses it with magisterial finality: 'Explanations associating it with certain pillars at the Exchange in Limerick and Bristol are too late to be of any authority in deciding the question.'

World Religions

A   The Jewish, Christian and Islamic belief that there is only one God.

B   The belief held by Hindus and many other ancient civilisations that there are many gods.

C   The first five books of the Old Testament.

D   Rabbinical writings on Jewish civil and religious laws that are not contained in the first five books of the Old Testament.

E   The first three Gospels of the New Testament, which have many similarities.

F   A chapter in the Koran.

G   A movement working towards greater unity between Christian churches.

H   All the gods of a people, or a temple in which all of them are honoured.

I   A mythological great hall in which Nordic warriors who have died heroically can drink and feast throughout eternity.

J   In Greek mythology, a place where the souls of the blessed are rewarded for their conduct during their lives on earth.

Clues

A   10 letters: *mon-------*

B   10 letters: *pol-------*

C   10 letters: *Pen-------*

D   6 letters: *Ta----*

E   2 words, 8, 7 letters: *Syn----- G------*

F   4 letters: *s---*

G   10 letters: *ecu-------*

H   8 letters: *Pan-----*

I   8 letters: *Val-----*

J   7 letters: *Ely----*

See page 54 for answers

Answers, Word Origins and Usage

A   **Monotheism**. *Adj:* **monotheistic**. Greek *monos* (single, alone) + *theos* (god).

B   **Polytheism**. Greek *polus* (many).

C   The **Pentateuch**. Greek *pente* (five) + *teukhos* (scroll). The five books are: Genesis, Exodus, Leviticus, Numbers and Deuteronomy.

D   The **Talmud**.

E   **Synoptic Gospels**. Greek *sun* (together) + *opsis* (view). The Gospels are: Matthew, Mark and Luke.

F   **Sura**. Arabic for 'step'.

G   **Ecumenical**. Greek *oikoumenikos* (the entire inhabited world).

H   **Pantheon**. Greek *pan* (all) + *theion* (holy).

I   **Valhalla**. Old Norse for 'Hall of the slain.'

J   **Elysium**. Also called the **Elysian Fields**.

Behind the Word

It may not be a comforting thought, but early Chancellors of the Exchequer counted the revenues of the realm in a way reminiscent of roulette croupiers in a casino. The practice began, under the Norman kings, of spreading a chequered cloth over a table so that it looked like an outsized chessboard, then stacking counters on the squares as an aid to financial calculations. The Old French for chessboard was *eschequier*, which soon anglicised itself into exchequer. The word **chancellor**, derived from the Latin *cancellers,* has come up in the world since Roman days. It used to mean the guardian of the space around an altar. Then it came to mean, in succession, a court secretary and secretary to the monarch. Today, the Lord Chancellor is at the head of the nation's legal system and the Chancellor of the Exchequer is the most powerful man in the land when it comes to deciding what taxes we should pay and how the money raised should be spent.

World Religions

A Refusal to accept the beliefs of a church – especially those laid down as dogma.

B Not in agreement with orthodox beliefs and teaching.

C The belief that there is an eternal struggle between God, represented by light, and Satan, represented by the dark.

D Sixteenth-century Christian sect that began in Zurich, rejected infant baptism and taught that the only baptism accepted in the scriptures was that of adults.

E The belief that Jesus, though the highest of created beings, was not divine.

F A fifth-century heresy holding that Jesus was two people in one body: one human, the other Divine.

G A crusade, conducted with great cruelty, against a heresy that swept through southern France in the 12th and 13th centuries.

H A tenth-to-fourteenth-century European sect that believed all matter was evil and they should therefore live as frugally as possible.

I The destruction of the world, as predicted in the biblical Book of Revelation; hence, any violent event of close to earth-shattering dimensions.

J The final battle between good and evil, followed by the Day of Judgement.

Clues

A 6 letters: *h*-----

B 9 letters: *het*------

C 11 letters: *Man*--------

D 11 letters: *Ana*--------

E 8 letters: *Ar*------

F 12 letters: *Nes*---------

G 2 words, 11 letters and 7: *Alb*-------- *C*------

H 9 letters: *Cat*------

I 10 letters: *Apo*-------

J 10 letters: *Arm*-------

See page 56 for answers

Answers, Word Origins and Usage

A **Heresy**. *Adj:* **heretical**. Somebody who rejects an officially approved belief: **heretic**. Greek *haeresis* (choice, sect).

B **Heterodox**. *Noun:* **heterodoxy**. Greek *heteros* (other) + *doxa* (opinion, notion).

C **Manichaeism**. Named after its founder, Manes (or Mani), a third-century Persian religious leader.

D **Anabaptists**. Greek *ana-* (again). Those baptised in infancy had to be baptised again.

E **Arianism**. Named after its founder, Arius (250–336). The doctrine was declared a heresy in AD 381.

F **Nestorianism**. Named after its founder, Nestorius, the fifth-century Patriarch of Constantinople.

G **Albigensian Crusade**. Named after Albiga, where the prohibited sect once flourished.

H **Catharism**. Adherents of the sect were also called **Albigensians**.

I **Apocalypse**. Greek *apokalupsis* (to uncover).

J **Armageddon**. Hebrew *Megiddo*, a mountainous region where many battles were fought.

World Religions

A   Jews whose ancestry can be traced to Spain or Portugal or who currently live in either of these countries.

B   Jews whose ancestry can be traced to Central or Eastern Europe or who currently live in these regions.

C   The dispersal of Jewish people over many countries, following such catastrophes as the Babylonian Captivity in the sixth century BC and the destruction of the Jerusalem Temple by the Romans in AD 70.

D   Muslims who believe that the true successor to Muhammad was his close companion, Abu Bakr, who became the first Caliph (religious and secular leader).

E   Muslims who believe that Muhammad's true successor was Ali, his cousin and son-in-law.

F   The buying or selling of ecclesiastical offices or pardons for sins.

G   The remission of punishment for a sin, given in return for money.

H   Charitable; concerned with the giving of alms.

I   A member of the class that was once known, under the Hindu caste system, as the Untouchables.

J   A member of Hinduism's highest caste.

Clues

A   8 letters: *Sep*-----

B   9 letters: *Ash*------

C   8 letters: *Dia*-----

D   5 letters: *Su*---

E   6 letters: *Sh*----

F   6 letters: *si*----

G   10 letters: *ind*-------

H   12 letters: *ele*---------

I   7 letters: *Har*----

J   7 letters: *Bra*----

See page 58 for answers

Answers, Word Origins and Usage

A **Sephardi**. *Adj:* **Sephardic**. Hebrew *Sapharadhi* (Spaniard).

B **Ashkenazi**. *Adj:* **Ashkenazic**. From Ashkenaz, a grandson of Noah.

C **Diaspora**. Greek *diaspeirein* (dispersal).

D **Sunni**. Arabic *Sunnah* (Muhammad's sayings and rulings on Islamic beliefs and duties).

E **Shiite**. Arabic. Also **Shi'a** (contraction of *Shiat Ali,* 'a follower of Ali').

F **Simony**. After Simon Magus, a Samaritan who offered money to St Peter and St John if they would grant him the power of conferring the Holy Spirit on whomever he pleased.

G **Indulgence**.

H **Eleemosynary**. Greek *eleemosune* (charitable).

I **Harijan**. Sanskrit *Hari* (dedicated to the god Vishnu) + *jana* (person). The new name was given at the behest of Mahatma Gandhi (1869–1948).

J **Brahman**. Also spelled **Brahmin**. Sanskrit for 'priest'. By tradition, priests were drawn from this group. In the USA the word Brahmin has come to mean a mature, well-educated, highly cultured person who can be relied on for sage advice.

The Man Who Was Far From Gruntled

A surprising number of words in the English language that begin with dis-, meaning 'not', do not work if that negating prefix is dropped. In P. G. Wodehouse's *The Code of the Woosters,* Bertie Wooster makes the remark: 'I could see that, if not disgruntled, he was far from being gruntled, so I tactfully changed the subject.' How many other words cannot survive having their *dis* taken away? A person can be dishevelled but not *shevelled*, distinguished but not *tinguishe*d, disdainful but not *dainful*, disgusting but not *gusting*. The search for a word that can live without its *dis* begins to seem hopeless, but there are a few exceptions to the rule. To be *barred* means much the same as disbarred, but it is far better to be *appointed* than to be disappointed.

Birds of a Feather

A COLLECTION OF:	CLUES
A Rooks	10 letters: *par-------*
B Crows	6 letters: *mu----*
C Ducks	5 letters: *fl---*
D Swans	4 letters: *h---*
E Geese	6 letters: *g-----*
F Eagles	11 letters: *con--------*
G Falcons	4 letters: *c---*
H Jays	5 letters: *pa---*
I Pigeons	5 letters: *f----*
J Doves	6 letters: *f-----*

See page 60 for answers

Answers, Word Origins and Usage

A A **parliament** of rooks. Alternative: a **clamour**.

B A **murder** of crows.

C A **flush** of ducks. Alternative: a **team**.

D A **herd** of swans. Alternative: a **bevy**.

E A **gaggle** of geese. Alternative: a **flock**.

F A **convocation** of eagles.

G A **cast** of falcons.

H A **party** of jays.

I A **flock** of pigeons. Alternative: a **flight**.

J A **flight** of doves. Alternative: a **dole**.

Behind the Word

In 1492, when Cardinal Rodrigo Borgia became Pope Alexander VI, it was already a tradition for Popes to appoint nephews (*nepote* in Italian) as cardinals, giving them the right to elect the successor. Pope Alexander went one better – or rather, one worse – and appointed his notorious son, Cesare Borgia. *Nepotismo*, the favouring of nephews in the Catholic Church, was not officially ended until 1692, when Pope Innocent XII issued a Bull against it. By that time, the word **nepotism** had found a wider meaning and a new home in the world of business. It now means showing favouritism to any family member when it comes to selection for a job or a promotion. Many companies have rules against practising nepotism, but family firms are exempt. They can build dynasties without being criticised, as can the children of famous actors – as long as the performance lives up to the promise.

Birds of a Feather

A COLLECTION OF:	CLUES
A Starlings	11 letters: *mur--------*
B Sparrows	7 letters: *qua----*
C Larks	10 letters: *ex--------*
D Nightingales	5 letters: *w----*
E Thrushes	8 letters: *mut-----*
F Plovers	12 letters: *con---------*
G Lapwings	6 letters: *de----*
H Magpies	6 letters: *ti----*
I Finches	9 letters: *tre------*
J Goldfinches	5 letters: *ch---*

See page 62 for answers

Answers, Word Origins and Usage

A   A **murmuration** of starlings.

B   A **quarrel** of sparrows. Alternative: **host**.

C   An **exaltation** of larks.

D   A **watch** of nightingales.

E   A **mutation** of thrushes.

F   A **congregation** of plovers. Alternative: a **wing**.

G   A **deceit** of lapwings.

H   A **tiding** of magpies.

I   A **trembling** of finches.

J   A **charm** of goldfinches.

Behind the Word

The Sophists were Greek philosophers in the fifth century BC
who began with the best of intentions but lost their way because
of the lure of riches. The earliest of them were seekers of truth,
wandering from city to city and making a living by sharing their
insights with audiences who were not only willing to pay, but
eager to do so. Among those who came to listen, however, were
many who were less concerned about the search for truth than
about finding ways to advance their careers. The more a Sophist
had to say about how to win arguments and influence people, the
higher the fees he could charge. The Greek word *sophos* (skilled,
clever) came to imply clever trickery. This is still the meaning of
sophistry today: a facility for putting forward arguments that
sound persuasive even though they may not ring true. The word
sophisticated, though it has the same roots, has kept enough
of the aura of the first sophists to hold on to respectability. A
sophisticated person – usually a woman – knows the ways of
the world but at the same time is looked up to as a role model
because of her elegance, refinement and self-assurance.

BIRDS OF A FEATHER

A COLLECTION OF:	CLUES
A Owls	5 letters: *st---*
B Ravens	10 letters: *un-------*
C Quails	4 letters: *b---*
D Snipe	4 letters: *w---*
E Teal	4 letters: *r---*
F Woodcock	4 letters: *f---*
G Partridges	5 letters: *c----*
H Grouse	5 letters: *c----*
I Seagulls	6 letters: *c-----*
J Penguins	8 letters: *ro-----*

See page 64 for answers

Answers, Word Origins and Usage

A A **stare** of owls. Alternative: a **parliament**.

B An **unkindness** of ravens.

C A **bevy** of quails. Alternative: a **covey**.

D A **wisp** of snipe. Alternative: a **whisper**.

E A **raft** of teal.

F A **fall** of woodcock.

G A **covey** of partridges.

H A **covey** of grouse.

I A **colony** of seagulls.

J A **rookery** of penguins. Alternative: a **colony**.

The Secret Language of Savile Row

Most men in need of a new suit will buy it off the peg. Those who can afford to splash out and are looking for a more perfect fit and a wider choice of cloth will go to a tailor, to be measured and fitted. They may well find that the person doing the measuring begins to mutter strange sets of initials: FS…SRB…DRS…and so forth. If this sounds like a code, that is precisely what it is – a code that avoids causing unnecessary embarrassment to a customer whose shape is not quite up to comparison with that of a Greek statue. FS means 'Forward Stomach'; SRB 'Slightly Round Back'; and DRS 'Dropped Right Shoulder'. These are relatively minor drawbacks that can easily be camouflaged. The acid test comes with BL (Bow Legs), and to make the cutter's job even harder, the code allows for increasing stages: BL1…BL2 …BL3.

The Law of the Land

A Public defamation in writing or in some other permanent form that unjustifiably injures somebody's reputation.

B Public defamation in speech or some other non-permanent form that unjustifiably injures somebody's reputation.

C A court order that prohibits somebody from taking a specified action.

D Evidence that does not bear directly on the facts of a case but points indirectly to an accused person's guilt or innocence.

E A signed statement, confirmed by an oath or the equivalent, which will be accepted by a court in the unavoidable absence of a witness.

F A writ demanding that somebody who has been arrested and imprisoned should be brought before a court for trial.

G Decision in a criminal court, that a case should be dropped.

H A judge's opinion, expressed in court, and that has no essential bearing on the case and is therefore not binding.

I An obligation, usually financial, under which a defendant is granted bail after agreeing to carry out a specified action, such as returning to court on a set date. If the obligation is not met, the bail money is liable to be forfeited.

J A time-waster, known for seeking to bring disputes into court for the sake of annoying defendants, rather than because the cases are well founded.

Clues

A 5 letters: *l----*

B 7 letters: *s------*

C 10 letters: *inj-------*

D 14 letters: *cir-----------*

E 9 letters: *aff------*

F 2 words, both 6 letters: *h----- c-----*

G 2 words, 5 letters and 8: *no--- pro-----*

H 2 words, both 6 letters: *ob---- di----*

I 12 letters: *rec---------*

J 2 words, 9 letters and 8: *vex------ lit-----*

See page 66 for answers

Word Origins and Usage

A   **Libel**. *Adj:* **libellous**.

B   **Slander**. *Adj: slanderous*.

C   **Injunction**. Latin *injunctus* (enjoin, command, direct forcefully).

D   **Circumstantial** evidence.

E   **Affidavit**. Latin *affidare* (to trust).

F   **Habeas corpus**. Latin for 'you shall have the body'. The right to be protected by the writ goes back to Magna Carta (1215).

G   **Nolle prosequi**. Latin for 'to be unwilling to pursue'. This decision does not rule the possibility of a fresh trial.

H   **Obiter dictum**. Latin for 'a remark made in passing'.

I   **Recognisance**. Old French *reconoistre* (to recognise).

J   **Vexatious litigant**.

The Law of the Land

A   The study of the principles and philosophy of law.

B   The right and power to apply the law; the range over which a legal system can exercise its authority.

C   A prison sentence that will be served at the same time as another sentence or sentences.

D   A prison sentence to be served after another sentence has reached its end.

E   Goods found floating at sea after being thrown overboard or following a shipwreck.

F   Goods that have been washed ashore or are found on the seabed after being thrown overboard.

G   Supplement to a will, adding revoking or explaining clauses.

H   A system of inheritance under which lands and titles are passed down to a firstborn son.

I   To accuse somebody of treason or some other crime against the State.

J   Incitement to rebel against the authority of the State.

Clues

A   13 letters: *jur----------*

B   12 letters: *jur---------*

C   10 letters: *con-------*

D   10 letters: *con-------*

E   7 letters: *fl-----*

F   6 letters: *j-----*

G   7 letters: *c------*

H   13 letters: *pri----------*

I   7 letters: *im-----*

J   8 letters: *se------*

See page 68 for answers

Answers, Word Origins and Usage

A **Jurisprudence**. Latin *jus* (law) + *prudentia* (knowledge, wisdom).

B **Jurisdiction**. Latin *jus* (law) + *dicere* (to say, declare).

C **Concurrent** sentence. Latin *concurrere* (run alongside, run together).

D **Consecutive** sentence. Latin *consequi* (follow up, follow closely).

E **Flotsam**. Memory-jogger: floating.

F **Jetsam**. Memory-jogger: jettisoned.

G **Codicil**. Latin *codicillus* (writing tablet, book).

H **Primogeniture**. Latin *primo* (first) + *genitura* (birth). In countries where primogeniture benefits only a son, moves are afoot to change 'firstborn son' to 'firstborn child'.

I **Impeach**. *Noun:* **impeachment**. Latin *impedicare* (to put in fetters). Example: *President Nixon resigned when he was threatened with impeachment over the Watergate scandal.*

J **Sedition**. *Adj:* **seditious**. Latin *sed* (apart) + *itio* (going).

Counting Sheep

These days counting sheep is little more than a last resort for insomniacs, but for hundreds of years ``before the Industrial Revolution permanently shifted the population balance between country and town it was a daily task of paramount importance.

Shepherds all over Britain had to count their flocks at regular intervals to make sure none had strayed, been stolen or taken by wolves. The numbers used for the count varied in different parts of the country but all were based on the language of an ancient Celtic tribe, the Brythons. A typical sequence ran along these lines:

1	2	3	4	5
Yan	Tan	Tethera	Pethera	Pimp
6	7	8	9	10
Sethera	Lethera	Hovera	Covera	Dick
11	12	13	14	15
Yanadick	Tanadick	Tetheradick	Petheradick	Bumfit
16	17	18	19	20
Yanabumfit	Tanabumfit	Tetherabumfit	Petherabumfit	Jigger

Round Britain Word Tour

Regional dialects, having survived some serious attempts to eradicate them, remain useful pointers to where a speaker was brought up. Try your hand, whether left or right, at untangling the list below and matching the word to the place.

LEFT-HANDEDNESS		REGION	
A	corrie-fisted	1	Wales
B	cloddy-handed	2	North East
C	clicky-handed	3	Glasgow
D	coggy-handed	4	Scottish Borders
E	cuddy-wifter	5	Liverpool
F	gallock-handed	6	The Midlands
G	cack-handed	7	Cornwall
H	keggy-handed	8	Yorkshire

See page 68 for answers

Answers

A4 B3 C7 D1 E2 F8 G5 H6

Signs of the Times

Chaucer: Midwife of the English Language

Modern English was born in the fourteenth century, and Geoffrey Chaucer (1342–1400) was the midwife. A glossary or long study is needed to read much of his work, but there are snatches in which every word can be fully understood. Here he is, writing about his love of books:

> On bokes for to rede I me delyte,
> To hem yive feyth and ful credence,
> And in myn herte have hem in reverence...

The spelling may seem a little quaint, but allow for that, change the *y* in *yive* to *g* and any difficulties vanish. Chaucer's vocabulary was based on a mixture of Old English, Norman French, Latin and Norse, spiced with a dash of the emerging world of commerce, travel and diplomacy. He gave currency to such words as *ambassador, bribe, argument* and *outrageous,* as well as words concerned with more spiritual matters, such as *vertu* (virtue), *inspired* and *pilgrimage*. The Hundred Years War between England and France broke out just a few years before he was born, and gunpowder made its appearance on the battlefield. It is no surprise that a man who lived in such troubled times was the first English writer to mention *artillery*.

The Heavens Above

A   The lowest level of the atmosphere, from sea level to about 15 km (9.3 miles) above the Earth. As altitude increases, the temperature falls. Near its upper boundary, high-flying planes take advantage of the powerful winds of the jet stream.

B   A boundary layer, only 20–50 m (66–164 ft) thick, where the temperature is constant.

C   The level of the atmosphere that contains ozone, which shields much of the planet against life-destroying ultraviolet radiation from the sun. It extends from *c.* 15–50 km (9–31 miles) above Earth.

D   Atmospheric layer from 50–80 km (31–50 miles) above the Earth, where temperatures drop to -100°C (-148°F).

E   The next layer, up, where intense solar radiation breaks down molecules of gas and strips atoms of their electrons, producing ions.

F   The uppermost level of the atmosphere. Beyond it lies interplanetary Space.

G   Multicoloured display of lights in the night sky, seen in northern latitudes.

H   Multicoloured display of lights in the night sky, seen in southern latitudes.

I   Two brilliantly coloured belts of electrically charged particles that are trapped by Earth's magnetic field.

J   The most distant point reached in an orbit around Earth.

Clues

A   11 letters: *tro--------*

B   10 letters: *tro-------*

C   12 letters: *str---------*

D   Initial plus 5 letters: *- l----*

E   10 letters: *io--------*

F   13 letters: *mag----------*

G   2 words, 6 letters and 8:

    A----- B-------

H   2 words, 6 letters and 9:

    A----- A---------

I   3 words, 3, 5 and 5 letters:

    V--- A---- b----

J   6 letters: *ap----*

See page 72 for answers

Answers, Word Origins and Usage

A **Troposphere**. Greek *tropos* (change of temperature).

B **Tropopause**.

C **Stratosphere**. *Adj:* **stratospheric**. Latin *stratus* (something laid down, stretched out).

D **D layer**. Formerly known as the **Mesosphere**. Greek *mesos* (middle).

E **Ionosphere**.

F **Magnetosphere**.

G **Aurora Borealis** – the Northern Lights.

H **Aurora Australis** – the Southern Lights.

I **Van Allen belts**. They are named after the American scientist who identified them.

J **Apogee**. Greek *apo* (away from) + *gaia* (Earth).

The Aussie Way with Words

Australians have added a welcome mix of vigour, humour and irreverence to the language. A man with a beer belly has a *verandah*, a timid surfboard learner is a *shark biscuit,* to vomit is to *chunder* or to take a *technicolour yawn*. A hooligan is a *larrikin*, a deodorant is a *pommie shower*, somebody who shows a certain reluctance to stand his round of drinks is a *wowser*, and a slow-witted person is a *drongo* or a *galah*. In politics, Aussie invective is more than able to stand comparison with Denis Healey's description of being criticised by Sir Geoffrey Howe as *rather like being savaged by a dead sheep*. Paul Keating, when he was Australia's Prime Minister, described one of his opponents as *a shiver, waiting for a spine to run up*. Small wonder that Australian cricketers are so good at the kind of ruthless banter they invented, known as *sledging*.

Parlez-vous Français?

A A disagreement or an unexpected mishap that can cause a setback to plans.

B The spirit of pride, loyalty and 'all for one, one for all' that binds a group together.

C Witty retort to an insult, but one that comes to mind too late to be delivered.

D For want of a better choice or proposal.

E A decision taken or a deed done without asking for agreement either from partners or from opponents.

F The more things change, the more they stay the same.

G A tip, for somebody who has provided good service.

H Don't protest your innocence too much, for he who excuses himself accuses himself.

I A second home or dwelling place of any kind, acquired for the sake of convenience.

J An innate understanding of how to behave in all circumstances and work one's way through setbacks and difficulties.

K An area or region occupied by a group that is different in origin and characteristics from the surrounding group.

NOTE: In the following clues for the French language quizzes, two words are counted as one if linked by tacking an apostrophe onto the initial letter of the first word, as in *d'état*.

Clues

A 11 letters: *co*---------

B 3 words, 6, 2 and 5 letters: *e*----- *d*- *e*----

C 2 words, 6 letters and 9: *e*----- *d*--------

D 3 words, 5, 2 and 5 letters: *f*---- *d*- *m*----

E 2 words, 4 letters and 8: *f*--- *a*-------

F 8 words, 4, 2, 6, 4, 4, 2, 4 and 5 letters:
    p--- *c*- *c*-----, *p*--- *c'*--- *l*- *m*--- *c*----

G 9 letters: *p*--------

H 3 words, 3, 7 and 7 letters: *q*-- *s'*------ *s'*------

I 3 words, 4, 1 and 5 letters: *p*--- - *t*----

J 2 words, 6 letters and 5: *s*----- *f*----

K 7 letters: *e*------

See page 74 for answers

Answers, Word Origins and Usage

A **Contretemps**. Literally, 'against time'. Originally a term used in fencing to indicate a thrust made at the wrong moment.

B **Esprit de corps**.

C **Esprit d'escalier**. Literally, 'the spirit or inspiration of the staircase' – that is, outside the room where it should have been made.

D **Faute de mieux**.

E **Fait accompli**. Usually announced with a strong implication that the deed cannot be undone.

F **Plus ça change, plus c'est la même chose**. Often abbreviated to **plus ça change…**

G **Pourboire**. Literally, 'for a drink', in the sense of 'have one on me'.

H **Qui s'excuse s'accuse**.

I **Pied à terre**. Literally, 'a foot on the ground'.

J **Savoir faire**. Literally, 'know how to do'.

K **Enclave**. Often designating an area occupied by troops from a foreign country.

Parlez-vous Français?

A   Something that has to be done because of a rule or a long-standing convention.

B   The best of the best.

C   A painting that deceptively looks as real as a three-dimensional object.

D   A plot that leads to the swift overthrow of a government and the seizure of power by a new group.

E   A gifted young person whose ideas and behaviour cause consternation to those who take a more conventional approach to life.

F   A free hand; unrestricted authority.

G   To solve a mystery, look for the woman.

H   A person or thing that is intensely disliked, causes annoyance and is avoided whenever possible.

I   Deliberately shock people who set great store by moderation and conventional behaviour.

J   Let's get back to our main subject.

NOTE: In the following clues for the French language quizzes two words are counted as one if they are linked by tacking an apostrophe onto the initial letter of the first word, as in *d'état*.

Clues

A   2 words, 2 letters and 6:
    d- r-----

B   5 words, 2, 5, 2, 2 and 5 letters:
    l- c---- d- l- c----

C   2 words, 6 letters and 5:
    t----- l'o---

D   2 words, 4 letters and 5:
    c--- d'----

E   2 words, 6 letters and 8:
    e----- t-------

F   2 words, 5 letters and 7:
    c---- b------

G   3 words, 8, 2 and 5 letters:
    c------- l- f----

H   2 words, 4 letters and 5:
    b--- n----

I   3 words, 6, 3 and 9 letters:
    e----- l-- b--------

J   4 words, 8, 1, 3 and 7 letters:
    r------- à n-- m------

See page 76 for answers

Answers, Word Origins and Usage

A **De rigeur**. Literally, 'because of strictness'.

B **La crème de la crème**. Literally, 'the cream of the cream'.

C **Trompe l'oeil**. Literally, 'deceives the eye'.

D **Coup d'état**: 'a stroke of State'. The phrase is also applicable to a sudden seizure of power in a boardroom or any large enterprise.

E **Enfant terrible**. Literally, 'terrible child'.

F **Carte blanche**: 'blank card'.

G **Cherchez la femme**.

H **Bête noire**: 'black beast'.

I **Épater les bourgeois**: 'to amaze the middle classes'.

J **Revenons à nos moutons**. Literally, 'Let's get back to our sheep' – a line from a play.

Movie Memories

Scriptwriters are not given to wasting words, and some of their lines can have as much impact as images on the screen. Who said the following, and in which film?

A   Fasten your seat belts – it's going to be a bumpy night.

B   Top of the world, Ma!

C   Nobody's perfect.

D   ...it doesn't take much to see that the problems of three little people don't amount to a hill of beans in this crazy world.

E   Tomorrow is another day.

F   In Italy for thirty years under the Borgias they had warfare, terror, murder and bloodshed, but they produced Michelangelo, Leonardo da Vinci and the Renaissance. In Switzerland they had brotherly love, they had 500 years of democracy and peace – and what did they produce? The cuckoo clock.

G   I am Spartacus!

H   One morning I shot an elephant in my pyjamas. How he got into my pyjamas I'll never know.

See page 78 for answers

Answers

A   Bette Davis, in *All About Eve*.

B   James Cagney, in *White Heat*.

C   Joe E. Brown, in *Some Like It Hot*.

D   Humphrey Bogart, in *Casablanca*.

E   Vivien Leigh, in *Gone With the Wind*.

F   Orson Welles, in *The Third Man*.

G   Tony Curtis, echoed by a small army of extras, in *Spartacus*.

H   Groucho Marx, in *Animal Crackers*.

Parlez-vous Français?

A   Each person to his or her own taste.

B   Is it not so?

C   A marriage or love affair in which three people live together rather than the conventional two.

D   Love at first sight.

E   A final blow or shot, to put a badly wounded person or animal out of their misery.

F   An affectionate and often amusing nickname.

G   That elusive something; a distinctive quality that cannot be pinned down.

H   Unable, through injury, illness or exhaustion, to take any further part in a struggle.

I   An assumed name, adopted by a writer.

J   The tradition that people of high rank have responsibilities as well as privileges.

NOTE: In the following clues for the French language quizzes two words are counted as one if linked by tacking an apostrophe onto the initial letter of the first word, as in *d'état*.

Clues

A   4 words, 6, 1, 3 and 4 letters: *c----- a s-- g---*

B   2 words, 4, 2 and 3 letters: *n--- c- p—*

C   3 words, 6, 1 and 5 letters: *m----- a t----*

D   3 words: 4, 2 and 6 letters: *c--- d- f-----*

E   3 words: 4, 2 and 5 letters: *c--- d- g----*

F   9 letters: *s--------*

G   4 words, 2, 2, 4 and 4 letters: *j- n- s--- q---*

H   3 words, 4, 2 and 6 letters: *h--- d- c-----*

I   3 words, 3, 2 and 5 letters: *n-- d- p----*

J   2 words, 8 letters and 6: *n------- o-----*

See page 80 for answers

Answers, Word Origins and Usage

A **Chacun à son goût**.

B **N'est-ce pas?**

C **Ménage à trois**. Literally, 'three-person household'.

D **Coup de foudre**: 'thunderbolt, stroke of lightning'.

E **Coup de grâce**. Literally, 'stroke of mercy'.

F **Sobriquet**. Also spelled **soubriquet**. Literally, 'a tap under the chin'.

G **Je ne sais quoi**: 'I don't know what'.

H **Hors de combat**: 'out of the fight'.

I **Nom de plume**: 'a pen name'.

J **Noblesse oblige**: 'nobility brings obligations'.

Anagrams: Switching Letters to Make a Point

The best anagrams have a touch of truth and more than a touch of wit about them. When, in the 1920s, the French poet André Breton rearranged the letters in Salvador Dalí's name to spell Avida Dollars it may have been from envy, for his fellow Surrealist Dalí never seemed to have any trouble in finding a ready market for his paintings. Whatever the motivation, if there were an Anagram Olympics, Breton would win the gold medal. A silver might go to whoever turned William Shakespeare into 'I am a weakish speller'. It might have been a gold, but there used to be various ways of spelling Shakespeare's name, all of them acceptable, and this probably made life a little easier for anagram compilers. And the bronze? What about 'Flit on, cheering angel' for Florence Nightingale?

Some anagrams are puzzling until explained. Why did a television production team entitle their science fiction/fantasy series *Torchwood*? The answer is that it was a spin-off from the highly successful series, *Doctor Who*, and when they needed a working title somebody had a flash of inspiration. *Torchwood* not only sounds intriguing but it is also an anagram of *Doctor Who*. So why look any further for the new title?

Sprechen Sie Deutsch?

A number of German words that have found a place in English dictionaries and the English language are still, as it were, wearing their lederhosen. Here are some of them:

A   The spirit of the Age.

B   An all-pervading sense of sadness and pessimism about the state of the world.

C   Years devoted to travel; Germany's Romantic equivalent of a gap year.

D   An atmosphere creating geniality, cosiness and good cheer.

E   An attempt to overthrow a government by force.

F   The double of a living person, especially one in the form of an apparition that haunts that person.

G   A recurring theme, especially in a Wagnerian opera, associated with a person or idea.

H   Songs and ballads for voice and piano, as in the works of Schubert and Schumann.

Clues

A   9 letters: *z*--------

B   11 letters: *w*----------

C   11 letters: *w*----------

D   13 letters: *gem*----------

E   6 letters: *p*-----

F   12 letters: *do*----------

G   9 letters: *l*--------

H   6 letters: *l*-----

See page 82 for answers

Answers, Word Origins and Usage

A **Zeitgeist**.

B **Weltschmerz**. Literally, 'World sorrow'.

C **Wanderjahre**: 'Years of travel'.

D **Gemütlichkeit**. *Adj:* **gemütlich**.

E **Putsch**: 'A thrust'.

F **Doppelgänger**: 'Double goer, double walker'.

G **Leitmotif**. Also spelled **leitmotiv**. 'Leading motif '.

H **Lieder**.

Signs of the Times

Shakespeare's Gifts

Seldom has history seen such an explosion of energy, ideas and language as the one that transformed English society during the reign of Elizabeth I, from 1558 to 1603. Her subjects were peasants and farmers, merchants and scholars, poets and painters, playwrights, pirates and explorers, bankers and lawyers, courtiers and craftsmen, fortune hunters and dynasty-builders. With so many sources to draw upon, the language expanded at a near furious rate. Shakespeare alone is estimated to have had a vocabulary of around 20,000 words and to have introduced nearly 3,000 new ones. He may or may not have been the first to use them, but there is no doubt that he was the first to put them record. *Accommodation, untutored, frugal, obscene, reliant, pedant, premeditated, reliant, unturned* are among the army of words that made their first recorded appearance in his plays and sonnets.

When it comes to phrase-making, Shakespeare is even more impressive. He created hundreds of expressions that have passed into the everyday language: *Salad days...One fell swoop... Pound of flesh...Foregone conclusion... Infinite variety... Love is blind...It is a wise father that knows his own child... Green-eyed jealousy...Blinking idiot...This scepter'd Isle... More honour'd in the breach than the observance...All our yesterdays...*The audiences of the day, too, played their part. It is a tribute to them that they could relish such a phrase as Lady Macbeth's *the multitudinous seas incarnadine.* What would most television viewers make of it today?

Behind the Word

According to Dr Johnson – and who would dare to contradict the great lexicographer? – the word **bankrupt** goes back to the days of the Italian Renaissance. During that explosion of inventiveness in so many directions, the Italians were the foremost bankers of Europe. Money dealers in Florence and other fabulously wealthy cities would lay out what they had to offer on *banca* (tables) and if a dealer ran so short that he was unable to meet his debts his table would be *rotta* (broken). The unfortunate man would then be *bancarotta*.

Sprechen Sie Deutsch?

A Enthusiastic and uncritical support for a person or an idea.

B Building castles in the air; daydreams.

C Malicious pleasure derived from the failures and misfortunes of other people, especially those who are supposed to be friends.

D An eighteenth-century literary movement opposed to any attempt to restrain the free, unfettered display of motions.

E A nineteenth-century nationalist movement proclaiming that Germany had a right to colonise land to the East, although it was already occupied by Slavs.

F Territory beyone a country's existing frontiers to allow for a nation's expansion and full development.

G A school of art and architecture founded in Germany in 1919 by Walter Gropius that combined meticulous design with craftsmanship.

H A struggle for control between religious and civil authorities.

Clues

A 10 letters: *sch-------*

B 9 letters: *tr-------*

C 13 letters: *sch----------*

D 3 words, 5, 3 and 5 letters: *St--- u-- D----*

E 3 words, 5, 4 and 5 letters: *D---- n--- O----*

F 9 letters: *l---------*

G 7 letters: *b------*

H 11 letters: *Kul--------*

See page 86 for answers

Answers, Word Origins and Usage

A **Schwämerei**.

B **Traumerei**. From *traum* (dream).

C **Schadenfreude**: *schaden* (harm) + *freude* (joy)'.

D **Sturm und Drang**: 'Storm and stress'.

E **Drang nach Osten**: 'The drive to the East'.

F **Lebensraum**: 'Living space'.

G **Bauhaus**: 'House of Architecture'.

H **Kulturkampf**: 'A struggle between cultures'. The original Kulturkampf (1872–87) was between Bismarck and the Roman Catholic Church.

Polari Comes Out of the Closet

Before permissiveness came into fashion in the Sixties, gay men risked being sent to prison. To keep their secret from those likely to report them to the police they developed a secret language: **Polari**. Here is an example: *Vader the boni omi with the naff barnet*. Translation: 'Look at that handsome man with the deplorable haircut.' It was not a very well-kept secret, for Polari was broadcast, even if not fully understood, by every radio in the land in the comedy show *Round the Horne*.

Kenneth Horne, the star of the show, would regularly drop in for a chat with two camp characters, Julian and Sandy, who referred to legs as *lallies*, eyes as *minces*, faces as *eeks*, a woman as a *palone*, tough guys of either sex as *butch*, anything they admired as *bona*, and anything they thought of as common or in poor taste as *naff*. Their highest form of praise and delight was *fantabulusa!* and they pretended to be shocked by any proposal that was even slightly daring with cries of *oo – bold!* Then, the encounter with Kenneth Horne over, they would *troll off*.

Polari draws from many sources, including Cockney rhyming slang and the language of the travelling fairground. Other words in its vocabulary include *tush* (backside), *zhoosh* (to fix, improve or smarten up), *sharpy* (policeman) and *cottaging* (using a public lavatory as a meeting place). Its greatest triumph, and one that can still provoke an occasional protest, was to commandeer the word *gay*.

Cut Through Confusion

Words that sound alike, look alike or seem to point in the same direction do not necessarily share the same meaning. This quiz is designed to help anybody who has ever fallen into the trap of confusing confusables.

A   Concern over the worries, misfortunes and yearnings of other people, coupled with a desire to help them.

B   A close understanding of the feelings of other people, coupled with an ability to share those feelings.

C   To stumble, collapse or, in the case of a ship, to sink.

D   To move or set about a task awkwardly, clumsily and ineffectively.

E   A statement that is open to being interpreted more ways than one.

F   Being in two minds about something, each contradicting the other.

G   To refrain from doing something, however tempting that something may be.

H   An ancestor.

I   A warehouse or other place where goods may be stored for safe-keeping.

J   Not only a warehouse storing goods but also a place in which information is stored.

Clues

A   8 letters: *sym-----*

B   7 letters: *emp----*

C   7 letters: *fou----*

D   8 letters: *flo-----*

E   9 letters: *amb------*

F   10 letters: *amb-------*

G   7 letters: *for----*

H   8 letters: *for-----*

I   10 letters: *dep-------*

J   10 letters: *rep-------*

See page 88 for answers

Answers, Word Origins and Usage

A **Sympathy**. *Adj:* **sympathetic**. Example: John had so much sympathy for victims of the tsunami that he devoted every moment he could spare to raising funds for them.

B **Empathy**. *Verb*: **empathise**. Example: Sarah empathised with Janet when her boyfriend walked out, because she had been through a similar episode herself.

C **Founder**. Example: Heavy seas battered our rust-bucket of a ship until she foundered, but the captain was still able to get the entire crew into a lifeboat.

D **Flounder**. Example: It should be easy enough to put together a flat-pack table, so why don't you stop floundering, read the instructions and get on with it?

E **Ambiguous**. *Noun:* **ambiguity**. Latin *ambiguus* (wandering around). Example: According to journalists, who always enjoy a good story, a newspaper once carried the ambiguous headline: MacArthur Flies Back to Front.

F **Ambivalent**. *Noun*: **ambivalence**. Example: John had an ambivalent attitude towards fast driving. He spoke against it in theory but never missed a chance to go over the limit if the road ahead seemed clear.

G **Forbear**. *Noun*: **forbearance.** Past tense: **forbore**. Example: Charles forbore to press home his advantage when his son lay the queen open to capture at chess, for after all the boy was only six years old and a beginner.

H **Forebear**. From a Scottish dialect word meaning 'somebody who has been before'.

I **Depository**. Example: When the Joneses went to live in France for a year they put their most valuable furniture into a depository for safe keeping.

J **Repository**. Example: Jowett's extensive reading and capacious memory made him a positive repository of information about the ancient Greeks.

The Language of Science

A   A subatomic particle that carries a negative electrical charge.

B   A subatomic particle that carries a positive electrical charge.

C   A subatomic particle that carries no electrical charge.

D   Atoms of the same element that contain equal numbers of protons but different numbers of neutrons.

E   Any of the different physical structures which a chemical element can take – as with carbon, which can form graphite, charcoal or diamond.

F   A substance which can speed up a chemical reaction without being consumed or altered itself.

G   A liquid solution or a gas in which tiny particles of matter are suspended, as in a pea-souper fog.

H   The slightly curved upper surface of liquid in a glass, tube or similar container.

I   A half shadow, occupying a region between full shadow and full light.

J   In chemistry, containing carbon. In the general language, completely natural and derived from living organisms, with nothing added that is artificial.

Clues

A   8 letters: *el------*

B   6 letters: *pr----*

C   7 letters: *ne-----*

D   7 letters: *is-----*

E   9 letters: *all------*

F   8 letters: *cat-----*

G   7 letters: *col----*

H   8 letters: *men-----*

I   8 letters: *pen-----*

J   7 letters: *or-----*

See page 90 for answers

Answers, Word Origins and Usage

A **Electron**. Memory-jogger: electricity.

B **Proton**. Greek *protos* (first).

C **Neutron**. Memory-jogger: neutral.

D **Isotope**.Greek *isos* (equal) + topos (place).

E **Allotrope**.Greek *allo* (altered, other) + *tropos* (turning away).

F **Catalyst**. Greek *kata* (down) + *luein* (release).

G **Colloid**. Greek *kolla* (glue).

H **Meniscus**. Greek *meniskos* (crescent, moon).

I **Penumbra**. Latin *paene* (half) + *umbra* (shadow).

J **Organic**. *Antonym*: **inorganic**. Gk. *organikos* (tool, implement, instrument).

Dodging the Blame

Nobody enjoys being embarrassed, and even less so does any nation. So unfortunate ailments get passed, in an international game of 'pass the parcel', to other countries. To an Englishman it's the Spanish pox – or at least it used to be. To a German it was the Polish disease; to a Pole the German disease; and to a Turk the Christian disease. And so on, with no country eager to blame itself. To a doctor, making a professional judgement rather than a jingoistic one, it is syphilis.

Cut Through Confusion

A An erroneous belief or impression that has no foundation in reality and is likely to lead to a wrong decision.

B A figment of the imagination, often when 'seeing' something that does not exist.

C Hard to pin down, to catch or to remember.

D To repeal a law or go back on a decision.

E To claim power and authority for oneself, with no outside justification.

F An arrangement that takes some of the sting out of misfortune by regular payments in advance, to establish a right to compensation if there is loss, damage or injury.

G An arrangement under which payments establish a right to compensation for events that are certain to happen. One such event is death, in which case the compensation would go to one's heirs.

H A statement that is open to being understood in many ways.

Clues

A 8 letters: *del-----*

B 8 letters: *ill-----*

C 7 letters: *el-----*

D 8 letters: *ab------*

E 8 letters: *arr-----*

F 9 letters: *ins------*

G 9 letters: *ass------*

H 9 letters: *amb------*

See page 92 for answers

Answers, Word Origins and Usage

A **Delusion.** *Adj*: delusive. Latin *deludere* (to deceive).

B **Illusion.** *Adj*: illusory. Latin *in* (towards) + *ludere* (to play).

C **Elusive.** Latin *eluere* (to wash out).

D **Abrogate.** Latin *ab* (away from) + *rogare* (to regulate, pass a law).

E **Arrogate.** Memory-jogger: arrogant.

F **Insurance.**

G **Assurance.**

H **Ambiguous.** Latin *ambi* (around, on both sides) + *agere* (to lead, drive).

Behind the Phrase

To be offered **Hobson's choice** is to be allowed no choice at all: you either take what is on offer or you go without. The phrase goes back to Thomas Hobson (1544–1631) who ran a livery stable in Cambridge, renting mounts to those who needed a gallop but had no access to a horse of their own. The customers always wanted the best horses, but Hobson had other ideas. He owned around 40 horses and believed it was good business to rotate them. Then there would be no danger of the best becoming worn out. Hobson made it a rule that would-be riders should take the horse he had deliberately placed in the stall nearest to the stable door. Those who insisted on a different choice were turned away with nothing.

Cut Through Confusion

A In a fighting mood; ready and eager to use violence or make war.

B Actually at war, or so aggressive and hostile that war is likely to break out.

C A process of reasoning by which conclusions are based on the application of well-understood general rules; reasoning from the general to the particular.

D A process of reasoning by which conclusions are reached on the evidence of particular instances; reasoning from the particular to the general.

E Individual, clearly defined and unlike anything else.

F So gifted or special in some other way as to stand out from the crowd.

G Unable to concentrate on important matters because one's attention has been attracted by something else.

H Overwhelmed by anxiety to the point of being agitated and unable to concentrate.

I Distracted, worried and inattentive.

Clues

A 9 letters: *bel------*

B 11 letters: *bel--------*

C 9 letters: *ded------*

D 9 letters: *ind------*

E 8 letters: *dis-----*

F 11 letters: *dis--------*

G 10 letters: *dis-------*

H 10 letters: *dis-------*

I 8 letters: *dis-----*

See page 94 for answers

Answers, Word Origins and Usage

A **Bellicose**. Latin *bellum* (war). Example: When Arthur had a few drinks inside him he was best avoided, because beer always made him bellicose.

B **Belligerent**. Latin *bellum* (war). Example: Without exception the belligerent powers longed for an end to the slaughter, but they all wanted peace on their own terms.

C **Deduction**. *Verb:* **deduce**. Latin *deducere* (to lead away). Example: Sherlock Holmes deduced that since a dog did not bark in the night it must have been familiar with the intruder.

D **Induction**. Latin *inducere* (to lead in). Example: Many of the world's fastest sprinters have been exposed as users of performance-enhancing drugs, but that does not give anybody grounds to assume, by a process of induction, that every record-breaking athlete, is a cheat.

E **Distinct**. Latin *distinguere* (to distinguish, set apart). Example: The moment that Matthew stepped through the door of the old cottage he had a distinct feeling of *déjà vu*.

F **Distinctive**. Example: The distinctive sound of the Glenn Miller orchestra owed as much to his use of saxophones as it did to his virtuosity on the trombone.

G **Distracted**. *Noun:* **distraction**. Latin *distrahere* (to pull apart). Example: Worried and inattentive Philippa had been an avid reader since childhood. At the age of nine, not even her favourite doll could distract her from *Wuthering Heights*.

H **Distraught**. The best man was far too distraught to keep up with the wedding service. He felt frantically in all his pockets, but no ring could he find.

I **Distrait**. Example: Bertie Wooster felt more than a little distrait when he discovered that Jeeves had somehow forgotten to pack the yellow waistcoat he was so proud of.

Quote or Misquote?

A Roll up that map. It will not be wanted again these ten years –
   William Pitt (1759–1806), who became Britain's Prime Minister
   at the age of twenty-four.

B The lights are going out all over Europe; we shall not see them lit
   again in our lifetime – Lord Grey (1862–1933), Britain's Foreign
   Secretary

C Go West, young man – Horace Greeley (1811–72), American editor

D Who's your fat friend? – Beau Brummell (1778–1840), referring
   to the Prince of Wales

E Television? The word is half Greek and half Latin. No good can
   come of it – *Manchester Guardian* editor C. P. Scott (1846–1932)

See page 96 for answers

Quotations check

A   Correct. The map in question was of Europe, and Pitt had just heard news of Napoleon's 1805 victory over the Austrians and Russians at Austerlitz. Pitt's prediction was accurate: Napoleon met his Waterloo ten years later.

B   Incorrect. Grey said 'lamps', not 'lights' as he gazed out of a Foreign Office window on the outbreak of the First World War.

C   Correct.

D   Correct.

E   Incorrect. C. P. Scott was scholar enough to say, 'half Latin and half Greek'.

Behind the Phrase

Any Irishman who has the eloquence and wit to hold the attention not just of a few friends but of a large audience – and there are many who fit this description – is said to have kissed the **Blarney stone**. This is a triangular stone on the battlements of Blarney Castle, near Cork, and kissing it demands both suppleness and a head for heights. You have to lean out head down, with your legs and feet well secured. The single word blarney has come to mean talk spiced not just with wit but also with flattery and sometimes with an intention to mislead. According to legend, this goes back to Cormac McCarthy, a sixteenth-century Lord of Blarney, who used his considerable powers of persuasion to resist an English attempt to take over some of his territorial rights. Queen Elizabeth is believed to have commented: 'It's all blarney. What he says he never means.'

Cut Through Confusion

A To use words in a way that implies something that goes beyond their literal meaning.

B To indicate, be a sign of, reveal or suggest.

C Taking it for granted that one's actions or statements are correct and therefore acceptable.

D Taking it for granted that an action, a statement or a conclusion is correct even though it may be founded on little more than guesswork.

E A group of students, meeting to discuss their subject and exchange ideas, under the guidance of a tutor.

F A college where aspiring priests, ministers and rabbis are trained.

G Behaviour that is scandalous, shocking and unashamedly so.

H Behaviour that is unapologetically offensive.

I A sign that is taken as a forecast of future events, whether they be good or calamitous.

J A tool with a screw point, used for boring holes in wood.

Clues

A 7 letters: *co*-----

B 6 letters: *de*----

C 10 letters: *ass*-------

D 11 letters: *pre*--------

E 7 letters: *sem*----

F 8 letters: *sem*-----

G 8 letters: *fl*------

H 7 letters: *bl*-----

I 5 letters: *au*---

J 5 letters: *au*---

See page 98 for answers

Answers, Word Origins and Usage

A   **Connote**. Latin *conotare* (to mark in addition, mark together). Example: The fact that Jimmy went straight to the missing purse connoted either that he had the nose of a bloodhound or that he had put it there.

B   **Denote**. Latin *de* (completely) + *nota* (mark, indicate). Example: Harold was a notorious name-dropper – a habit which clearly denotes a lack of self-confidence.

C   **Assumption**. *Verb:* **assume**. Latin *ad* (before) + *sumere* (to take). Example: John never carried printed cards because he assumed that all the people who mattered knew him and all those who didn't know him didn't matter.

D   **Presumption**. *Verb:* **presume**. *Adj:* **presumptuous**. Latin *prae* (before, in advance) + *sumere* (to take). Example: Doctor Livingstone, I presume?

E   **Seminar**. Latin *seminarium* (seed plot). Example: Geoffrey enjoyed attending seminars because they gave him a chance to show how widely he had read.

F   **Seminary**. A student: **seminarian**. Latin *seminarium* (seed plot). Example: Father Patrick, who was trained in a Jesuit seminary, was hard to defeat in an argument.

G   **Flagrant**. Latin *flagrare* (to blaze). Example: The execution of Nurse Edith Cavell in 1915 horrified the British public, who regarded it as a flagrant miscarriage of justice.

H   **Blatant**. Example: The witness showed a blatant disregard for the truth that the judge had to remind him of the penalties for perjury. The word 'blatant' was probably invented by the Elizabethan poet Edmund Spenser to describe a thousand-tongued monster.

I   **Augur**. *Noun:* **augury**. Example: It augurs well for our little enterprise that the supermarkets are beginning to show a keen interest. The word can also mean a Roman religious official who foretold the future by such means as examining the entrails of birds.

J   **Auger**. Middle English *nauger*. In later centuries the *n* was dropped, in the same way that the snake once called *a nadder* became *an adder*.

Cut Through Confusion

A A number or extent that is endless and boundless.

B Strictly, too tiny to be measured, weighed or calculated; loosely, something extremely small.

C To compel somebody either to act in a certain way or to refrain from action.

D To check, repress, hold oneself or somebody else back from taking action.

E To agree with a proposal, suggestion or decision.

F To agree or give permission after being asked.

G A concise summary of a career, a book, a report, an investigation and suchlike, covering all the essential facts.

H A brief outline of the plot of a book or a play.

I To assert that an accusation is unfounded and untrue.

J To prove that an accusation is unfounded and untrue.

K To reject an accusation or deny a line of argument emphatically, often with a touch of anger.

Clues

A   8 letters: *inf-----*
B   13 letters: *in-----------*
C   9 letters: *con------*
D   8 letters: *res-----*
E   6 letters: *as----*
F   7 letters: *con----*
G   6 letters: *pr----*
H   8 letters: *syn-----*
I   4 letters: *d---*
J   6 letters: *re----*
K   9 letters: *rep------*

See page 100 for answers

Answers, Word Origins and Usage

A **Infinite**. *Noun:* **infinity**. Latin *in* (not) + *finire* (to limit, set bounds). It has been said that genius is an infinite capacity for taking pains, but this takes something essential out of the meaning of 'genius'.

B **Infinitesimal**. Quarks are mysterious and infinitesimally minute sub-atomic particles, believed to play a part in the creation of an atom's protons and neutrons.

C **Constrain**. *Noun:* **constraint**. Latin *constringere* (to draw tightly together). Example: The batsman was plainly out lbw but he refused to walk until constrained to do so by a disapproving eye from his captain.

D **Restrain**. *Noun:* **restraint**. Latin *restringere* (to restrict). Example: By a supreme effort of will, David restrained himself from calling the umpire a cheat.

E **Assent**. Latin *adsentire* (to join in, share a feeling). Example: Margaret was in one of her rare good moods, so she readily assented to the idea of holding a family get-together.

F **Consent**. Latin *consentire* (to feel the same way). Example: Paul readily gave consent when Martin asked for his daughter's hand in marriage and was happy that the formalities had been observed.

G **Precis**. Latin *praecidere* (to omit, cut out the front part). Memory-jogger: precise.

H **Synopsis**. Greek *sun* (together) + *opsis* (view).

I **Deny**.

J **Refute**.

K **Repudiate**. Latin *repudiare* (to cast off). Example: After being shocked by the sight of homeless people sleeping on the streets, whatever the weather, Sally repudiated a good many of her former views.

Signs of the Times

The King James Bible

The King James Bible is a cathedral built with blocks of words and phrases rather than stone. It is also a rare instance of a committee creating a work that lies beyond the genius of any single person. Remarkably, it arose from the deliberations of no fewer than six committees, based in Oxford, Cambridge and Westminster. Their members were all leading scholars and for the most part men in holy orders. They had been charged by King James I with producing a translation of the Bible that would carry its message to his subjects from lecterns and pulpits throughout the land. What soon became known as the Authorised Version was printed in 1611, at a time when the English language was reaching the heights. One reason why the King James version has left an imperishable mark is that its compilers followed a rule of reading their translations to each other. This gave the written word all the power and much of the simplicity of the spoken word. Among hundreds of phrases that have the power to stay in the mind and have been absorbed into the general language are:

A land flowing with milk and honey

Am I my brother's keeper?

The fat of the land

Cast thy bread upon the waters

Eye for eye, tooth for tooth

The stars in their courses

All flesh is grass

Let my people go

Though your sins be scarlet they shall be as white as snow

Every valley shall be exalted

Out of the strong came forth sweetness

The apple of his eye

For they shall see eye to eye

A dreamer of dreams

He smote them hip and thigh

They have sown the wind and they shall reap the whirlwind

The parting of the ways

Beat your swords into ploughshares

Let us now praise famous men

Generation of vipers

Man shall not live by bread alone

A man after his own heart

Blessed are the peacemakers

Blessed are the meek, for they shall inherit the earth

How are the mighty fallen!

The salt of the earth

The people arose as one man

Man is born into trouble as the sparks fly upward

Cast into outer darkness

Whited sepulchres

Weeping and wailing and gnashing of teeth

He that is not with me is against me

Consider the lilies of the field, how they grow; they toil not, neither do they spin

Gird up thy loins

I am escaped with the skin of my teeth...Neither do men put new wines into old bottles

Go to the ant, thou sluggard

A soft answer turneth away wrath

Physician, heal thyself

The race is not to the swift

A prophet is not without honour, save in his own country

And if the blind lead the blind both shall fall into the ditch

He passed by on the other side

It is easier for a camel to go through the eye of a needle than for a rich man to enter into the kingdom of God

If a house be divided against itself that house cannot stand.

Judge not, and ye shall not be judged

Go and do thou likewise

The wages of sin is death

Render therefore unto Caesar the things which are Caesar's; and unto God the things that are God's

It is better to marry than to burn

It is more blessed to give than to receive

For now we see through a glass, darkly

O death, where is thy sting? O grave, where is thy victory

Suffer fools gladly

Whatsoever a man soweth, that shall he also reap

I have fought a good fight

Unto the pure, all things are pure

A foolish man, which built his house upon the sand

All flesh is grass

The parting of the ways

And, perhaps surprisingly to many who are not Biblical scholars: GOD SAVE THE KING!

Cut Through Confusion

A   Presenting or suggesting a scene that will delight the eye; as pretty as a picture.

B   A story that tells of the triumphs and disasters of romantic adventurers and likeable rogues.

C   A line making the boundary of a shape or area.

D   A mathematical term, concerned with constants and variables which, because it sounds scientific, has been poached on behalf of the general language to mean a way of defining the scope and limits of an activity or process.

E   Heavy artillery and the military equipment needed to keep it ready for action.

F   An order or command, issued by a recognised authority.

G   A person who is undergoing instruction to become a priest, minister, rabbi or Buddhist monk.

H   A number indicating quantity: one, two, three, fifty, and so on.

I   A number indicating position in a list or series: first, second, third, fifti-eth and so on.

Clues

A   11 letters: *pic*--------

B   10 letters: *pic*-------

C   9 letters: *per*------

D   9 letters: *par*------

E   8 letters: *ord*-----

F   9 letters: *ord*------

G   8 letters: *ord*-----

H   8 letters: *car*-----

I   7 letters: *ord*----

See page 104 for answers

Answers, Word Origins and Usage

A **Picturesque**. William Wordsworth found the riverside view from Westminster Bridge so compelling, so picturesque that he wrote: *'Earth has not anything to show more fair.'*

B **Picaresque**. Spanish *picaro* (rogue). *Don Quixote*, believed to have been written in prison in the closing years of the sixteenth century, is rightly regarded as the world's greatest picaresque novel.

C **Perimeter**. Greek *peri* (around, enclosing) + *metron* (measure). Example: It took the best part of a day for the duke to ride around the perimeter of his estate.

D **Parameter**. Greek *para* (alongside) + *metron* (measure). Example: Simon felt distinctly uneasy, knowing that hacking into telephone conversations lay well beyond the parameters of his job description.

E **Ordnance**. Latin *ordinare* (to arrange in order). Memory-jogger: Ordnance Survey. Its maps were drawn up by the Army as an essential part of defence preparations.

F **Ordinance**. Latin *ordinare* (to arrange in order).

G **Ordinand**. Latin *ordinare* (to arrange, put in order). Memory-jogger: ordain.

H **Cardinal** number. Latin *cardinalis* (principal).

I **Ordinal** number. Latin *ordinare* (to arrange in order).

Behind the Phrase

Why should 'Break a leg' be the traditional way of wishing that an actor will give an outstanding performance and thrill the audience? This theatrical superstition began when a leg was actually broken on stage – the leg of the assassin John Wilkes Booth. The American Civil War was all but over, after four years of hard fighting, and on the night of 14 April 1865, President Lincoln felt relaxed enough to go to Ford's Theatre in Washington to see the play *Our American Cousin*. Booth, a half-crazed supporter of the defeated South, entered the President's unguarded box and shot him in the head. He then jumped down to the stage, breaking a leg but still managing to shout, 'Sic Semper Tyrannis!' (So end all traitors) and to flee. Twelve days later he was cornered, hiding in a barn. Either Booth shot himself or he was killed in the gunfight. Why these events, from which came nothing good, should be associated with a phrase intended to give encouragement is a little obscure, but it may be because there has never been a more sensational event on any stage in the world.

The Menacing World of Orwell's Newspeak

In his novel, *Nineteen Eighty-Four*, George Orwell conjures up a nightmare world in which a totalitarian regime stays in power by keeping the population under constant observation and by controlling the language. The rulers believe that if there are no words with which to express or even think about subversive ideas it will be impossible to plan subversion. In the land of Oceania, the ruling party sets out to abolish dangerous words or strip them of unapproved meanings. The word 'free', for example, survives only in a statement such as 'the dog is free from fleas'.

Language is forced into a straitjacket by a severe reduction in vocabulary and by a radical simplification of grammar. 'Dark' becomes *unlight*, 'bad' becomes *ungood,* and 'warm' is changed to *uncold*. If emphasis is needed, Newspeak falls back on *pluscold* and *doublepluscold*. The tenses are simplified into babytalk, so that the past tense of 'steal' is *stealed*, that of 'swim' becomes *swimmed* and the past of 'think' is *thinked*. Plurals are dragooned into line, with *mans* instead of 'two men', *two oxes* rather than 'two oxen', *lifes* in place of 'lives' and so on.

As might be expected, *goodthink* is an approved word, while language that might remind people of better days is condemned as *oldthink*. Anybody suspected by *Thinkpol* (the Thought Police) of *thoughtcrime* can expect to be liquidated or at best be sent to a *joycamp*. There is a form of self-censorship, called *crimestop*, by means of which those on the verge of a dangerous thought can switch their minds to safer topics. Orwell gives the name *prolefeed* to what he condemns as 'the rubbishy entertainment and spurious news which the Party handed out to the masses'.

It seems ironical, given Orwell's love of language, that some of the phrases for which he is best remembered have taken on meanings far removed from his intentions. In his novel *1984*, the people of Oceania are constantly reminded, by enormous posters and through their television screens, that BIG BROTHER IS WATCHING YOU. Today, people in their millions are switching on their sets to watch *Big Brother*.

Cut Through Confusion

A   Solidly built; a considerable number, effect or impact.

B   To provide proof in support of a claim or assertion.

C   A road, a speech, an excuse that is full of twists and turns.

D   Extremely painful, mentally or physically, often both.

E   A well thought-out overall plan, which, if it works, can lead to success in warfare, business, politics or personal relationships.

F   The use of skills and manoeuvres to achieve an immediate goal, especially but not exclusively in battle.

G   Something that brings an advantage or serves one's interests, sometimes with a whiff of unfairness.

H   To speed up a process.

I   Lacking both physical and mental vitality; benumbed. In the case of animals, in a state of hibernation.

J   Swollen, bloated; language that is cloyingly ornate and too dense to read for pleasure.

Clues

A   11 letters: *sub--------*

B   11 letters: *sub--------*

C   8 letters: *tor-----*

D   9 letters: *tor------,*

E   8 letters: *str-----*

F   7 letters: *tac----*

G   9 letters: *exp------*

H   8 letters: *exp----*

I   6 letters: *to----*

J   6 letters: *tu----*

See page 108 for answers

Answers, Word Origins and Usage

A   **Substantial**. Latin *substare* (to stand up). Example: Philip backed three winners on the trot, so he ended the day cockahoop having made a substantial profit.

B   **Substantive**. Latin *substantia* (something that exists). Example: The case for building a new airport was certainly substantive but it still roused determined opposition.

C   **Tortuous**. Latin *tortus* (a twist). Example: The road over the mountain is tortuous in places and it's worth being extra careful on those sections.

D   **Torturous**. Latin *tortus* (twisted). Memory-jogger: torture.

E   **Strategy**. *Adj* **strategic**. *An act in support of a strategy:* **stratagem**. Greek *strategos* (a general). Example: Germany's strategy in the early months of the First World War was based on the Schlieffen Plan, which called for a swift victory over France before turning East to face the Russians.

F   **Tactics**. *Adj:* **tactical**. Greek *tattein* (to form up, ready for battle).

G   **Expedient**. Latin *expedire* (to make ready). Example: Gilbert decided it was not an expedient time to let his partners know he was preparing to leave the company.

H   **Expedite**. *Adj:* **expeditious**. Latin *expidere* (to free the feet). Example: The peace talks had been dragging on for three years yet neither side seemed eager to expedite them.

I   **Torpid**. *Noun:* **torpidity**. Latin *torpere* (to feel stiff). Example: The heatwave had lasted three weeks and the entire family were feeling increasingly torpid every day.

J   **Turgid**. *Noun:* **turgidity**. Latin *turgere* (to swell). Example: Jones is such a pompous man, how could you expect him to be anything other than a turgid letter-writer?

Quote or Misquote?

A   He would say that, wouldn't he? – Mandy Rice-Davies

B   A modest little man, with much to be modest about – Winston Churchill on Clement Attlee

C   If Kitchener was not a great man, he was at least a great poster – Margot Asquith

D   Come up and see me sometime – Mae West

E   Candy is dandy. But liquor is quicker – Ogden Nash

F   No one would remember the Good Samaritan if he'd only had good intentions. He had money as well – Margaret Thatcher

See page 110 for answers

Quotations check

A   Incorrect. Ms Rice-Davies was responding to a question from the judge at a trial connected with the 1963 Profumo scandal. Asked whether she knew that Lord Astor had told the police her allegations were absolutely untrue, she replied simply, 'He would, wouldn't he?'

B   Correct.

C   Correct.

D   Incorrect. What Mae West said, in the 1933 film *She Done Him Wrong*, was: 'Why don't you come up some time and see me?'

E   Correct.

F   Correct.

Behind the Phrase

It is unlikely that Queen Marie Antoinette ever used the words for which she is best remembered: 'Let them eat cake.' The story goes that this was her response when she was told there was no bread for the starving people of Paris, but, whoever said it, the English version of the callous-sounding response is a mistranslation. The phrase in its original French refers to the egg-based pastry *brioche*, not to *pain* (bread). More importantly, it has also been attributed to other unpopular French queens, especially those who were not born on French soil. Marie Antoinette, as well as being notorious for her frivolity and extravagance, was Austrian, the daughter of Emperor Francis I. The same phrase was attributed to Queen Maria Theresa, a Spanish princess who was married to France's Sun King, Louis XIV, ninety-five years before Marie Antoinette was born. It is more than probable that 'Let them eat cake' was simply a brilliantly effective off-the-shelf item of political invective, ready for use when France had an unpopular foreign-born queen.

Approaching the End

A   Fleeting; disappearing gradually and in some danger of vanishing completely.

B   Living or lasting for only a brief time.

C   Temporary; passing; of short duration.

D   Fallen into disuse.

E   Perishable; subject to the frailty that comes with age.

F   Suffering from the mental and physical disabilities associated with extreme old age.

G   The final scene of a play, last chapter of a book and so forth, in which the plot is unravelled.

H   The forgiveness of sins; release from debts, obligations, punishment and so forth; in particular, a sacrament of the Roman Catholic Church.

Clues

A   10 letters: *eva*-------

B   9 letters: *eph*------

C   9 letters: *tra*------

D   9 letters: *des*------

E   8 letters: *cad*-----

F   6 letters: *s*-----

G   10 letters: *dén*-------

H   10 letters: *abs*-------

See page 112 for answers

Answers, Word Origins and Usage

A **Evanescent**. *Verb:* **evanesce**. Latin *vanescere* (to vanish, pass away). Example: The more time Rupert spent glued to the television, the more his chances of winning a scholarship began to look evanescent.

B **Ephemeral**. *Plural noun:* **ephemera**. Greek *epi* (on) + *hemera* (day). Example: As ephemeral as a mayfly which emerges from its nymph stage to live, mate and die in a single day.

C **Transient**. *Noun:* **transience**. *Alternative choice:* **transitory**. Latin *trans* (over) + *ire* (to go). Example: We had a transient friendship, which ended when Vicky married and went to live abroad.

D **Desuetude**. Latin *de* (reversal, undoing) + *suescere* (to become accustomed to). Example: Martin's bike had fallen into such a state of desuetude that it looked as if only the rust was holding it together.

E **Caducity**. Latin *cadere* (to fall). Example: Geoffrey watched his diet and joined a fitness club, for he refused to give into the approach of caducity.

F **Senile**. *Noun:* **senility**. Latin *senex* (old man). Memory-jogger: senior.

G **Dénouement**. Latin *nodus* (knot). Example: The stage is littered with corpses in the dénouement of *Hamlet*.

H **Absolution**. *Verb:* **absolve**. Latin *absolvere* (to free from).

Music Has Charms

A   The slow movement of a symphony.

B   A joyful, lively movement in a symphony.

C   Instruction to play in rapid tempo.

D   Music that is slow and serious.

E   Music for a slow, stately dance that was popular in the sixteenth century among the nobility.

F   A gradual slowing down in tempo.

G   An instruction to play at a moderate tempo.

H   A tuneful, song-like composition, often written for the violin or piano.

I   A sharp, crisp style with each note distinctly separate from its neighbours.

J   A gradual increase in the volume and intensity of sound.

K   A murmuring style of music produced by chimes and other percussion instruments, played in Java and other parts of the East Indies.

Clues

A   6 letters: *a-----*

B   7 letters: *sch----*

C   7 letters: *all----*

D   5 letters: *l----*

E   6 letters: *pav---*

F   11 letters: *ral--------*

G   7 letters: *and----*

H   6 letters: *son---*

I   8 letters: *sta-----*

J   9 letters: *cre------*

K   7 letters: *gam----*

See page 114 for answers

Answers, Word Origins and Usage

A **Adagio**. Italian for 'at ease'.

B **Scherzo**. Germanic *scherzen* (to jump for joy, jest).

C **Allegro**. Italian for 'lively'.

D **Largo**. Italian for 'broad'.

E **Pavane**. From an old Italian dance – the *danza pavanna* (dance of Padua).

F **Rallentando**. Italian *rallentare* (to relax).

G **Andante**. Italian *andare* (to go).

H **Sonata.** Italian *sonare* (to sound). Memory-jogger: song-like.

I **Staccato**. Italian *staccare* (to detach).

J **Crescendo**. Italian for 'increasing'. Often taken wrongly to mean a culmination or peak of loudness.

K **Gamelan**.

Round Britain Word Tour

Many of the terms for 'friend' are in widespread use: pal, chum, mucker, buddy and the overused mate (which can be resented if the closeness it implies does not exist). There is also a rich vein of local words:

DIALECT WORD	REGION
Acker	West Country
Skin; La	Liverpool (Scouse)
Butty	Wales
Bor	East Anglia
Marra	Northumbria
Kidda	North East (Geordie)

Music Has Charms

A   Unaccompanied and sometimes improvised passage in a concerto, in which the soloist is able to display a virtuoso's skills.

B   A sliding from note to note, as when fingers are moved swiftly along the keys of a piano.

C   A passage of music or an entire composition that calls for a smooth, flowing style.

D   The combination and harmonisation within a piece of music of two or more melodies.

E   Notes produced on a stringed instrument by plucking rather than by a bow.

F   A form of musical composition, much used by J. S. Bach, in which a melody is repeated in varied ways.

G   A way of changing the traditional rhythm by switching the accent from the expected strong beat to what would otherwise be a weak beat; offbeat.

H   Music that has not been written or rehearsed.

I   A grace note, usually one step in the musical scale above the note which it decorates.

J   All the notes that make up a chord, played in fast succession.

K   A device in opera and oratorio by means of which narrative information is given in the style of normal speech but with some musical support.

Clues

A   7 letters: *cad----*

B   9 letters: *gli------*

C   6 letters: *le----*

D   12 letters: *cou---------*

E   9 letters: *piz------*

F   5 letters: *f----*

G   10 letters: *syn-------*

H   8 letters: *imp-----*

I   12 letters: *app---------*

J   8 letters: *arp-----*

K   10 letters: *rec-------*

See page 116 for answers

Answers, Word Origins and Usage

A **Cadenza**.

B **Glissando**. Memory-jogger: glide

C **Legato**. Italian for 'continuous'.

D **Counterpoint**.

E **Pizzicato**. Italian *pizzicare* (to pluck).

F **Fugue**.

G **Syncopated**. Greek *sunkoptein* (to chop up). Memory-jogger: *Syncopated Rhythm* (song title).

H **Impromptu**. Memory-jogger: improvised.

I **Appoggiatura**. Italian *appoggiare* (to lean on).

J **Arpeggio**. Memory-jogger: harp.

K **Recitative**. Memory-jogger: recitation.

Round Britain Word Tour

An alley is an alley. But not always, and not everywhere.

DIALECT WORD	REGION
Backsie	West Country
Gennel, Snicket	Midlands
Ginnel, Entry	Lancashire
Jigger	Liverpool
Snicker	Yorkshire
Twittens	Sussex

The Greek Prefix Epi-

The Greek *epi-* prefix has given many English words a push start into existence because it is so versatile. It can mean 'upon', 'above' or 'in addition to', according to the context.

A   The very essence or embodiment of a person or an idea.

B   The revelation of a divine presence or the sudden recognition of an extraordinary event. Christian festival that commemorates the adoration of the newly born Jesus by the Three Wise Men.

C   A plant that grows on another plant, depending on it only for support, not for nourishment.

D   Having both male and female characteristics; effeminate.

E   A term used to describe a person or thing, often in a disparaging way.

F   An inscription on a statue, or one at the start of a book, setting out its theme.

G   Philosophical study of knowledge; inquiry into how we know what we think we know.

H   A term used in astronomy and in mechanics to denote a small circle that revolves around the circumference of a larger circle.

I   A person noted for refined tastes in food and wine.

J   A second-rater, devoted to a master but lacking the master's talent.

Clues

A   7 letters: *epi----*

B   8 letters: *epi-----*

C   8 letters: *epi-----*

D   7 letters: *epi----*

E   7 letters: *epi----*

F   8 letters: *epi-----*

G   12 letters: *epi---------*

H   8 letters: *epi-----*

I   7 letters: *epi----*

J   6 letters: *epi---*

See page 118 for answers

Answers, Word Origins and Usage

A   **Epitome**. *Verb*: **epitomise**. Greek *epi* + *temnein* (to cut). Example: Beau Brummel was the epitome of style in Regency England.

B   **Epiphany**. Greek *epi* + *phainein* (to show, reveal). Example: George had always thought of himself as being rather slow to learn, so it was a kind of epiphany for him when he learned he had been awarded a first-class degree.

C   **Epiphyte**. *Adj:* **epyphytic**. Greek + *phuton* (plant). Example: Whether you like the sight of ivy on a tree or not, it is an epiphyte and does no harm – unless, of course, it becomes so heavy that it brings the tree down.

D   **Epicene**. Greek *epi* + *koinos* (in common). Example: Who is that epicene youth leaning against the mantelpiece?

E   **Epithet**. Greek *epi* + *tithenai* (to place, put). Example: Janet called Harry a coward, but that was a mild epithet compared with some of the words she used once she got into her stride.

F   **Epigraph**. Greek *epi* + *graphein* (to write).

G   **Epistemology**. *Adj:* **epistemological**. Practitioner: **epistemologist**. Greek *epi* + *histanai* (to stand, place) + *logos* (word, speech).

H   **Epicycle**. *Adj:* **epicyclic**. Greek *epi* + *kuklos* (circle).

I   **Epicure**. *Adj:* **epicurean.** After the Greek philosopher Epicurus (341–270 BC) who taught that life should be lived in a way that avoided anxiety and pain. He was later misrepresented as advocating a life devoted to the active pursuit of luxury and pleasure, particularly regarding food and wine, and this view of his teachings prevailed.

J   **Epigon**. The Greek *epigonoi* were the sons of the seven heroes who attacked Thebes and passed into fable as the Seven Against Thebes. Their sons attacked the same city but did not emerge with the same glory.

Samuel Johnson Calls the Language to Order

Samuel Johnson (1709–84) was not the first man to compile a dictionary of English, but he set a style and a standard that were not surpassed until the emergence in 1889 of the *Oxford English Dictionary*, the product of a small army of philologists under the inspired editorship of the Scotsman James Murray. Johnson, who once said that no man but a blockhead ever wrote except for money, turned to dictionary making at the request of a group of booksellers and publishers. They offered more than £1,500 as an inducement, but however much he needed the money, Johnson had an even stronger motivation. While we look back on the language of the eighteenth century with reverence, Johnson saw much to criticise. 'Wherever I turned my view,' he wrote in his preface, 'there was perplexity to be disentangled and confusion to be regulated.'

In 1755, after nine years of solid work, his *Dictionary of the English Language* was published. Packed with quotations that supported the definitions, it was a sensational success. Some entries are written in what has become regarded as the typical Johnsonian style – the sort of language that seems in urgent need of a second dictionary to explain itself. For example, a *cough* is 'a convulsion of the lungs, vellicated by some sharp serosity'. *Network* is defined as 'any thing reticulated or decussated at equal distances, with interstices between the intersections'. Others are models of directness and simplicity. *Justice* is 'the virtue by which we give every man what is his due'. A *chairman* is 'the president of an assembly'. A *biographer* is 'a writer of lives' and a *blunderbuss* is defined as 'a gun that is charged with many bullets, so that, without any exact aim, there is a chance of hitting the mark'.

At times, Johnson reveals his prejudices. The most famous instance is his definition of *oats* as 'a grain which in England is generally given to horses, but in Scotland supports the people'. The most bitter, arising from the way Lord Chesterfield snubbed his request for sponsorship, is *patron*: '…commonly a wretch who supports with insolence and is paid with flattery'. The most poignant is *lexicographer*: 'A writer of dictionaries; a harmless drudge'. Then there is *monsieur*: 'A term of reproach for a Frenchman', and *garliceater*: 'a mean fellow'. His definition of a *lizard* as 'an animal resembling a serpent, with legs added to it' may lack precision but this is balanced by the fact that some of the words in his dictionary might with advantage be restored to the language. For example, *bedpresser*: 'a heavy lazy fellow'. Disarmingly, Johnson confesses to 'a few wild blunders and risible absurdities from which no work of such multiplicity was ever free'. These are few indeed. Taken as a whole, Dr Johnson (he was awarded an honorary degree at Oxford) made a contribution to the language that was immense.

Signs of the Times

The Sixteenth Century

A handful of years before the dawn of the sixteenth century, Columbus laid eyes on a New World. Within a remarkably short time, the Old World was exploring new knowledge and discovering foods, plants and animals, new poets and playwrights, new ways of living and, inevitably, fighting new wars. Among the words that entered the English language in the this century from around the world were: *atlas*, *archipelago*, *delta*, *canoe*, *cannibal*, *colony*, *puritan*, *barrister*, *banana*, *potato*, *tomato*, *caviar*, *coffee*, *tobacco*, *alligator*, *hippopotamus*, *turkey*, *genius*, *sonnet*, *grovel*, *haughty*, *aristocrat*, *renegade*, *bandit*, *violin*, *diary*, *conjugal*, *honeymoon*, *loyal*, *bullet*, *arsenal*, *calibre*, *decoy*, *explode* and *mutiny*.

Turning Back

A   The act of going back on a promise; changing a decision; withdrawing an accusation.

B   Something that recalls past events and experiences.

C   The return to an earlier habit or pattern of behaviour, and usually not one that is to anybody's benefit.

D   To bring a dying person or a vanishing dream back to life.

E   Somebody who habitually breaks the law or misbehaves in other ways and appears to be beyond reform.

F   Looking back in contemplation of bygone events, attitudes and achievements; a payment or other benefit that comes at an agreed time after the event that led to it.

G   To vomit partly digested food; hence, to repeat something that had been taught but not fully absorbed.

H   To take a step backward in one's plans or projects, making them less likely to succeed.

I   A criminal who carries on breaking the law after being released from jail.

J   To sum up the main points of a speech, plan, set of proposals and the like.

Clues

A   10 letters: *ret-------*

B   12 letters: *rem---------*

C   9 letters: *rev------*

D   11 letters: *res--------*

E   9 letters: *rep------*

F   13 letters: *ret----------*

G   11 letters: *reg--------*

H   10 letters: *ret-------*

I   10 letters: *rec-------*

J   12 letters: *rec---------*

See page 122 for answers

Answers, Word Origins and Usage

A **Retraction**. *Verb*: **retract**. Latin *re* (back, again) + *trahere* (to draw). Example: The buyer discovered that a better house was for sale at a cheaper price, but it was too late to retract because he had already signed a contract.

B **Reminiscence**. *Adj*: **reminiscent**. Latin *reminisci* (recollect). Example: For Marcel Proust the taste of a madeleine opened up a world of reminiscences.

C **Reversion**. *Adj*: **reversionary**. Latin *re* (back, again) + *vertere* (to turn). Example: By a praiseworthy effort of will, Brian stopped drinking for nearly a year but when he lost his job he reverted to type.

D **Resuscitate**. *Noun*: **resuscitation**. Latin *re* (back) + *suscitare* (to raise). Example: A lucky 18-1 win in the third race resuscitated Danny's hopes that he would be able to pay off the most pressing of his debts.

E **Reprobate**. *Noun*: **reprobation**. Latin *re* (back, against) + *probare* (to test). Often used jokingly: You little reprobate, you! I'll have your hide!

F **Retrospective**. *Nouns*: **retrospect, retrospection**. Latin *retro* (backwards) + *specere* (to look). Example: In retrospect it became clear to Andrew that he not made a good career decision when he threatened to resign.

G **Regurgitate**. Latin *re* (back) + *gurgitare* (flood, pour back). The word has an important extended meaning too: Archie got low marks in his English exam because he made no attempt to express his own feelings but simply regurgitated what he had been told.

H **Retrogress**. *Noun*: **retrogression**. *Adj*: **retrogressive**. Latin *retro* (backwards) + *gradus* (a step).

I **Recidivist**. *The condition*: recidivism. Latin *re* (back) + *cadere* (to fall).

J **Recapitulate**. *Noun*: **recapitulation**. *Abbreviated form*: **recap**. Latin *caput* (head).

Turning Back

A Said of an action or comment that is shameful and deserves a rebuke.

B Said of a sound, a deed or an action that reverberates beyond its initial impact.

C Stubbornly refusing to cooperate, yield to authority or accept guidance,

D The withdrawal of permission, repeal of a law or cancellation of privileges.

E To give something in return: good for good or tit for tat.

F Something so clever that it is difficult for anybody who is not an expert or a professional in the subject to understand it.

G Imbued with the power to bring back pleasant memories.

H A way of reacting to an accusation by making a counter accusation.

I Something, usually undesirable, that breaks out again after a period of dormancy.

Clues

A   13 letters: *rep----------*

B   8 letters: *res-----*

C   12 letters: *rec---------*

D   10 letters: *rev-------*

E   11 letters: *rec--------*

F   9 letters: *rec------*

G   8 letters: *red------*

H   13 letters: *rec----------*

I   13 letters: *rec----------*

See page 124 for answers

Answers, Word Origins and Usage

A **Reprehensible**. *Verb:* **reprehend**. *Noun:* **reprehension**. Latin *reprehendere* (to rebuke).

B **Resonant**. *Verb:* **resonate**. *Noun:* **resonance**. Latin *resonare* (to resound). Example: The exploits of the cockleshell heroes resonated far beyond the shores of their native land. Memory-jogger: resounding.

C **Recalcitrant**. *Noun:* **recalcitrance**. Latin *recalcitrare* (to kick back with the heels). Example: These recalcitrant corns of mine look as if they are going to keep me out of the cricket team this season.

D **Revocation**. *Noun:* **revoke**. Latin *re* (back) + *vocare* (to call). Example: Louis XIV's revocation of the Edict of Nantes had the result that thousands of Huguenots fled France, taking their skills with them.

E **Reciprocate**. *Noun:* **reciprocity**. *Adj:* **reciprocal**. Latin *reciprosus* (alternating). Example: Dorothy gave Allen a pair of gold cufflinks for his birthday and when hers came round he reciprocated with an engagement ring.

F **Recondite**. Latin *recondere* (to hide). Example: Joe sat down to read *A Short History of Time*, but found it so recondite that he gave up after the first few pages.

G **Redolent**. *Noun:* **redolence**. Latin *redolere* (fragrant). Example: The roaring fire inside and the deep snow outside were redolent of Christmases of long ago.

H **Recrimination**. *Verb:* **recriminate**. Latin *re* (in return) + *criminare* (to accuse). Example: Most family rows end up in mutual recriminations, which are pointless and best forgotten by both parties.

I **Recrudescence**. *Verb:* **recrudesce**. *Adj:* **recrudescent**. Latin *re* (again) + *crudescere* (to worsen). Example: There has been a recrudescence of ill feeling since half the workforce was sacked.

Signs of the Times

The Seventeenth Century

A country divided by civil war. A monarch overthrown and executed. Religious tensions. The relaxation of inhibitions during the reign of Charles II. And always the pursuit of new knowledge and new experiences. These were some of the themes that called for new words in the seventeenth century.

Among the new entrants: Roundhead, Ironside, adjutant, ammunition, barricade, bayonet, sabre, bomb, howitzer, recruit, colonel, tactics strategy, demagogue, puritan, iconoclast...pantomime, ventriloquist, ballet, drama, orchestra, euphemism, botany, decimal, logarithm, microscope, telescope, nebula, pendulum, sextant, gastric, haemorrhage, fossil, archives, diploma, agenda, enthusiasm, pandemonium, enthusiasm, diagnosis, gastric, tea, avocado, castanets, pagoda, dodo.

Round Britain Word Tour

Just as different regions all over the country have a plethora of their own locally brewed beers so they have their own words to describe the usual result of having one too many:

DIALECT WORD	REGION
Skimmished	West Country
Meddwyn	Wales
Kaylied	Lancashire
Catto'd	Yorkshire
Rubbered	Northern Ireland

Turning Back

A   Responding to the ideas and suggestions of other people, rather than taking the initiative oneself; also, reaching back to become effective from a date in the past.

B   Rethinking the basic structure of a company that is failing or not operating at full efficiency.

C   To protest, reprove or raise objections.

D   The reduction of costs.

E   Curved backwards.

F   The usually unwelcome consequence of an action, event or statement.

G   Well supplied; a feeling of fullness.

H   Shining brilliantly.

I   Something that revives memories, usually pleasant ones, of bygone events.

Clues

A   11 letters: *ret--------*

B   10 letters: *re-e-------*

C   11 letters: *rem--------*

D   12 letters: *ret---------*

E   9 letters: *rec------*

F   12 letters: *rep---------*

G   7 letters: *rep----*

H   9 letters: *ref------*

I   11 letters: *rem--------*

See page 128 for answers

Answers, Word Origins and Usage

A   **Retroactive**. Also **reactive**. Latin *retro* (backwards). *Antonym:* **proactive**.

B   **Re-engineer**. Example: The chairman reported that the re-engineering had been opposed by a number of directors but they were no longer with the company, and profits were now growing steadily.

C   **Remonstrate**. *Noun:* **remonstrance**. Latin *monstrum* (a warning, an omen).

D   **Retrenchment**. Old French *retrenchier* (to cut off). Gladstone summed up his political creed as: 'Peace, Retrenchment, Reform'.

E   **Recurvate**. Latin *re* (back) + *curvus* (curve). *Antonym:* **incurvate**.

F   **Repercussion**. *Adj:* **repercussive**. Latin *repercutare* (to bounce back). Example: Smithers was warned that plotting to oust his leader would have serious repercussions.

G   **Replete**. *Nouns:* **repletion**, **repleteness**. Latin *re* (again) + *plere* (to fill). Example: Basil waved away the offer of another slice of pie, saying he was already more than replete.

H   **Refulgent**. *Nouns:* **refulgence**, **refulgency**. *Adv:* **refulgently**. Latin *re* (back) + *fulgere* (to flash). Example: Van Gogh painted sunflowers in all their refulgent glory.

I   **Reminiscent**. *Noun:* **reminiscence**. Latin *reminisci* (to recollect). Example: The scenery around our new home is reminiscent of the North York Moors.

The Latin Prefix Ir-

A The belief that territory which once formed part of a nation but has since been lost should be restored or taken back by force.

B Something so obviously right that it cannot be denied or challenged.

C A decision, statement or course of action that cannot be reversed.

D A statement or deed so far beyond question or dispute that it cannot be proved wrong.

E Something that cannot be destroyed.

F Something that cannot be remedied or repaired.

G Something that must be done; unavoidable.

H A question or a problem to which there is no answer.

Clues

A 11 letters: *irr*--------

B 11 letters: *irr*--------

C 11 letters: *irr*--------

D 12 letters: *irr*---------

E 13 letters: *irr*----------

F 12 letters: *irr*---------

G 12 letters: *irr*---------

H 12 letters: *irr*---------

See page 130 for answers

Answers, Word Origins and Usage

A **Irredentism**. *Practitioner:* **irredentist**. Italian, from *Italia irredenta* (unredeemed Italy).

B **Irrecusable**. *Adv:* **irrecusably**. Latin *in* (not) + *recusabilis* (to be rejected).

C **Irrevocable**. *Noun:* **irrevocability**. *Adv:* **irrevocably**. Latin *in* (not) + *revocare* (to call back).

D **Irrefragable**. Latin *in* (not) + *refragari* (to oppose). Example: It is an irrefragable truth that allowing a fox into a hencoop will lead to mayhem.

E **Irrefrangible**. *Noun:* **irrefrangibility**. *Adv:* **irrefrangibly**. Latin *frangere* (to break). Example: There was an irrefrangible understanding between the Mountie and his horse.

F **Irremediable**. Memory-jogger: remedy.

G **Irremissible**. *Adj:* **irremissibility**. *Adv:* **irremissibly**. . Latin *ir* (not) + *remittere* (to release).

H **Irresolvable**. Also **irresoluble**. Latin *ir* (not) + *solvere* (to solve).

Opposites and Near Opposites

A   A conceited person who habitually puts self-interest ahead of the needs and interests of other people and is given to name-dropping and other forms of boasting.

B   A deep concern for the welfare of other people.

C   Somebody who dislikes, even hates, humankind.

D   The love of humankind, often expressed through charitable deeds on behalf of those needing help.

E   A man who dislikes women.

F   Decisions, actions and political allegiances that are based on long-held beliefs, doctrines and ideas.

G   Decisions and actions that are based on experience and practical considerations.

H   The theory that knowledge is derived through the senses and is based on experience and observation.

I   Shunning excess and exercising restraint, especially in matters of food and strong drink.

J   Somebody who acts without self-restraint in the pursuit of sensual pleasures.

Clues

A   7 letters: *eg-----*

B   8 letters: *al------*

C   13 letters: *mis----------*

D   12 letters: *phi---------*

E   10 letters: *mis-------*

F   11 letters: *ide--------*

G   9 letters: *pra------*

H   10 letters: *emp-------*

I   10 letters: *abs-------*

J   9 letters: *lib------*

See page 132 for answers

Answers, Word Origins and Usage

A **Egotist**. *Adj:* **egotistical**. *The condition:* **egotism**. Latin *ego* (I). The word **egoist**, which is more likely to be met in a technical context, has much the same meaning, but without the implication of boastfulness.

B **Altruism**. *Adj:* **altruistic**. *Practitioner:* **altruist**. Latin *alteri* (others).

C **Misanthropist**. *Adj:* **misanthropic**. *The practice:* **misanthropy**. Greek *misos* (hatred).

D **Philanthropy**. *Adj:* **philanthropic**. *Practitioner:* **philanthropist**. Greek *philos* (loving).

E **Misogynist**. *Adj:* **misogynistic**. *The condition:* **misogeny**. Greek *misos* (hatred) + *gunaik* (women).

F **Ideological**. *Noun:* **ideology**. Memory-jogger: Ideas. Aneurin Bevan, who began work in the pits at the age of thirteen, could not be shaken from his Socialist ideology.

G **Pragmatic**. *Noun:* **pragmatism**. Greek *pragma* (deed). Example: The council, hoping to save money, took a pragmatic decision and out-sourced refuse collection in the entire county.

H **Empiricism**. *Adjs:* **empirical**, **empiricist**. *Practitioner:* **empiricist**. Greek *empeirikos* (experience).

I **Abstemious**. *Noun:* **abstemiousness**. Latin *ab* (away from) + *temetum* (intoxicating drink). Memory-jogger: Abstain.

J **Libertine**. *Noun:* **libertinism**. Latin *liber* (free). Not to be confused with **libertarian** – somebody who upholds freedom of action and belief.

Opposites and Near Opposites

A   Somebody who pursues a life of luxury and voluptuous delights.

B   A person who seeks purification by renouncing worldly comforts and pleasures.

C   Somebody whose main interest in life is the pursuit of pleasure.

D   A proposition or argument backed by evidence and submitted for judgement.

E   The rebuttal, backed by evidence, of a proposition or argument.

F   The creation of a new and better proposition, arising from the clash of argument and counter-argument.

G   An input of fresh energy from a combination of different sources, creating a whole that is greater than the sum of its parts.

H   A marked absence of energy and enthusiasm, leading to poor results.

I   A greeting, sometimes elaborate and couched in flowery language and sometimes short and formal.

J   A leave-taking, usually at some length and mentioning warm memories.

Clues

A   8 letters: *syb-----*

B   7 letters: *asc----*

C   8 letters: *hed-----*

D   6 letters: *the---*

E   10 letters: *ant-------*

F   9 letters: *syn------*

G   7 letters: *syn----*

H   8 letters: *let-----*

I   10 letters: *sal-------*

J   11 letters: *val--------*

See page 134 for answers

Answers, Word Origins and Usage

A **Sybarite.** *Adjs:* **sybaritic**, **sybaritical**. From the ancient city of Sybaris, whose inhabitants were despised by the Greeks and regarded as somewhat unmanly because of their luxury-loving, self-indulgent way of life.

B **Ascetic.** *The practice:* **asceticism**. Greek *askein* (to exercise). St Simeon Stylites (AD 387–459), who lived for thirty years on top of a pillar, preaching to the crowds below, was nothing if not ascetic.

C **Hedonist.** *The practice:* **hedonism**. *Adj:* **hedonistic**. From the Greek for 'pleasure'.

D **Thesis.** Greek *tithenai* (lay down, place). Example: Olga astounded the professor with her controversial thesis about the origins of the Second World War.

E **Antithesis.** Greek *antithenai* (oppose) The word can also have the general meaning of 'direct opposite'. Example: What Charles was playing was, to my ear, the very antithesis of good music.

F **Synthesis.** *Verb:* **synthesise**. *Adj:* **synthetic**. Disraeli's Reform Act was a synthesis of Tory men and Liberal measures. 'Synthetic' also carries the meaning of 'man-made, rather than occurring in nature'.

G **Synergy.** *Adj:* **synergetic**. Greek *sunergos* (working together). Memory-jogger: energy. Example: The new manager introduced a little synergy into the company's operations, and not before time.

H **Lethargy.** *Adj:* **lethargic**. Latin *lethargia* (drowsiness).

I **Salutation.** *Adj:* **salutatory**. Latin *salutare* (to greet). The usual salutation in a letter used to begin: 'Dear——', but in emails this is usually replaced with 'Hi ——.'

J **Valediction.** *Adj:* **valedictory**. Latin *vale* (farewell) + *dicere* (to say).

Quote or Misquote?

A   Turn the other cheek – The King James Bible

B   Spare the rod and spoil the child – The King James Bible

C   Let him who is without sin cast the first stone – The King James Bible

D   Father, forgive them: for they know not what they do – The King James Bible

E   He who lives by the sword shall die by the sword – The King James Bible

See page 136 for answers

Quotations check

A   Misquote. The New Testament wording in the King James version is: 'Whosoever shall smite thee on thy right cheek, turn to him the other also.'

B   Misquote. The nearest the Authorised Version comes to this phrase is: 'He that spareth his rod hateth his son.'

C   Misquote. The correct quotation is: 'He who is without sin among you, let him first cast a stone at her.'

D   Correct quotation.

E   Misquote. The saying, in the gospel of St Matthew, is: 'All they that take the sword shall perish with the sword.'

Signs of the Times

1900–1914

Hindsight paints the early years of the twentieth century as being a golden age, a glorious period of peace and rising prosperity, when Britannia ruled the waves and along with them an empire on which the sun never set. It may well have been for some, but for many it was a period of squalor and social unrest. It was also a time of revolution in the arts and in the pursuit of knowledge about the universe. Here are some of the words and phrases that entered the language during this period:

Oedipus complex, psychoanalysis, libido, schizophrenia, Alzheimer's disease, anorexia, allergy, gamma ray, genetics, hormones, birth control, vitamin, addict, intelligentsia, nucleus, quantum theory, Cubism, suffragette, sabotage, hunger march, closed shop, propaganda, opinion poll, colour bar, segregation, vacuum cleaner, central heating, cinema, wireless, radio, television, jazz (music), motor bike, streamlined, aerodrome, pilot (of a plane), boy scout, girl guide.

Opposites and Near Opposites

A   An animal that has reverted to the wild, or a human being who has taken to living as if wild.

B   An animal species that once was wild but has been trained to serve humankind, or a human being who thoroughly enjoys all the comforts of home.

C   A bird that is born blind and helpless and so needs a fairly long stay in the nest after hatching.

D   A bird that reaches a relatively advanced stage inside the egg, and so is able to leave the nest soon after hatching.

E   Lacking courage; always keen to stay out of a fight or avoid a challenge.

F   Daring, fearless, not put off by fear or failure or the likelihood of danger.

G   The process by which nuclear power is created: the splitting of the nucleus of an atom, causing a massive release of energy.

H   A process that takes place inside the Sun, with light atomic nuclei forced under tremendous heat and pressure to combine into heavier nuclei, causing a massive release of energy.

Clues

A   5 letters: *f----*

B   12 letters: *dom---------*

C   10 letters: *nid-------*

D   10 letters: *nid-------*

E   13 letters: *pus----------*

F   8 letters: *int-----*

G   7 letters: *fis----*

H   6 letters: *fus---*

See page 138 for answers

Answers, Word Origins and Usage

A **Feral**. Latin *ferus* (wild). Example: Gangs of feral cats brought terror to the streets.

B **Domesticated**. *Noun:* **domesticity**. Latin *domus* (house, home). Example: All the breeds of sheep we know today are descended from those domesticated in the Middle East during the New Stone Age.

C **Nidicolous**. Latin *nidus* (nest) + *colere* (to inhabit). Memory-jogger: Nest-clinging.

D **Nidifugous**. Latin *nidus* (nest) + *fugere* (to leave, flee). Memory-jogger: Nest-fleeing.

E **Pusillanimous**. *Noun:* **pusillanimity**. Latin *pusillus* (very small) + *animus* (soul, mind).

F **Intrepid**. *Noun:* **intrepidity**. Latin *in* (not) + *trepidus* (alarmed). Example: The intrepid explorer ignored all warnings about crocodiles and waded deep into the river.

G **Fission**. *Adjs:* **fissile**, **fissiparous**. Latin *fissus* (split).

H **Fusion**. Latin *fusio* (melt). Memory-jogger: fuse.

Proverbs in Parallel

Here are some more instances of how folk wisdom offers the same advice, no matter how different the country it comes from.

French: If the horse is a gift you don't look at its teeth.
British: Never look a gift horse in the mouth.

French: The way to become a blacksmith is to work at the forge.
British: Practice makes perfect/the cobbler should stick to his last.

French: You can't teach an old monkey to make faces.
British: You can't teach an old dog new tricks.

French: Gifts from an enemy bring nothing but bad luck.
British: Beware of Greeks bearing gifts. (A reference to the wooden horse of Troy.)

Spoken in Anger

Most of the words in this list are broadly interchangeable, but look closer into their etymologies and more distinctive meanings should emerge.

A Vicious and caustic, as if the words had been soaked in acid.

B Bitter, ill-natured and heaped with accusations.

C To denounce violently, in a storm of anger.

D Hostile, venomous and intended to hurt.

E Abusive, bitter and insulting.

F Critical, mocking and intended to belittle.

G A 'tit for tat' battle, with each participant responding to an accusation with a counter attack.

H Motivated by malice and the desire to cause harm.

I Spreading false tales, often in coarse language, with the intention of destroying somebody's reputation.

J To defame; to cast doubt on the value of a person, an idea, or a performance.

Clues

A 9 letters: *vit------*

B 11 letters: *acr--------*

C 9 letters: *ful------*

D 8 letters: *vir-----*

E 12 letters: *vit---------*

F 8 letters: *der-----*

G 13 letters: *rec----------*

H 10 letters: *mal-------*

I 10 letters: *scu-------*

J 9 letters: *den------*

See page 140 for answers

Answers, Word Origins and Usage

A **Vitriolic**. Vitriol is an old word for sulphuric acid.

B **Acrimonious**. *Noun:* **acrimony**. Latin *acrimonia* (sharpness; originally a bitter taste or pungent smell).

C **Fulminate**. *Noun:* **fulmination**. Latin *fulmen* (lightning – hence a storm).

D **Virulent**. *Noun:* **virulence**. Latin *virus* (slime, poison).

E **Vituperative**. *Noun:* **vituperation**. Latin for 'dishonourable, blameworthy, shameful'.

F **Derisory**. Also **derisive**. *Noun:* **derision**. Latin *ridere* (to laugh at, mock). Example: When our house was put on sale the neighbours made us a bid, but their offer was derisively small.

G **Recrimination**. *Verb:* **recriminate**. *Adjs:* **recriminative, recriminatory**. Latin *recriminari* (accuse in return).

H **Malevolent**. *Noun:* **malevolence**. *Adv:* **malevolently**. Latin *malus* (bad) + *velle* (to will, wish).

I **Scurrilous**. *Noun:* **scurrility**. Latin *scurra* (buffoon).

J **Denigrate**. *Noun:* **denigration**. Latin *de* (completely) + *nigrare* (to blacken).

Medical Matters

A A doctor who is called in to look after patients when their regular doctor is not available.

B A doctor who specialises in childhood illnesses.

C Somebody who genuinely has an illness but is obsessed to an unreasonable degree by his or her state of health.

D A person who may or may not have an illness (apart from the condition described here) but is neurotically convinced that he or she is about to fall victim to one.

E A professional forecast of the likely course of a disease and the likely outcome of the treatment prescribed.

F A painkilling drug that does not cause the recipient to lose consciousness.

G A medication containing nothing that could either help or harm but which often leads to a good result because the patient believes it will work.

H A disease or any other defect that is present from birth.

I A persistent, long-lasting illness.

J Excessive sleepiness, capable in severe cases of causing people to fall asleep without warning, at awkward times.

Clues

A 5 letters: *l----*

B 13 letters: *pae----------*

C 14 letters: *val-----------*

D 13 letters: *hyp----------*

E 9 letters: *pro------*

F 9 letters: *ana------*

G 7 letters: *pl-----*

H 10 letters: *con-------*

I 7 letters: *chr----*

J 10 letters: *nar-------*

See page 142 for answers

Answers, Word Origins and Usage

A **Locus**. Latin *locum tenens* (holding a place).

B **Paediatrician**. *The study:* **paediatrics**. Greek *pais* (child) + *iatros* (physician).

C **Valetudinarian**. *Adj:* **valetudinary**. *The condition:* **valetudinarianism**. Latin *valetudinarius* (in poor health).

D **Hypochondriac**. *The condition:* **hypochondria**. From a Greek word for the part of the body just below the ribs, which was thought to be the seat of melancholy.

E **Prognosis**. *Adj:* **prognostic**. *Verb:* **prognosticate**. Latin *prognosticare* (to predict, know beforehand). The word is also used in non-medical contexts for any prediction, as in: The prognosis for the weather is that we can look forward to a barbecue summer.

F **Analgesic**. *Noun:* **analgesia**. Greek *an* (not) + *algein* (to feel pain).

G **Placebo**. *Plural:* **placeboes**. Latin *placere* (to please).

H **Congenital**. Latin *com* (together) + *genitus* (born). The word also has its non-medical applications: a congenital liar.

I **Chronic**. *Noun:* chronicity. *Adv:* **chronically**. Greek *khronos* (time). The word is also used outside medicine for any problem of long standing (a chronic inability to keep the files in order) and as a slang term for something or somebody who is useless and contemptible (I can't stand that man. He's chronic).

J **Narcolepsy**. *Adj:* **narcoleptic**. Greek *narco* (to make numb) + *lambanein* (to seize). The related word **narcotic** has come to mean not only a drug that induces drowsiness but also one that is habit-forming and changes behaviour for the worse.

Behind the Word

Perhaps the most ill-fated, **morganatic** marriage in history was that between Sophie von Chatkovata and Archduke Franz Ferdinand. While she was of noble birth, it was nowhere near noble enough for her to be considered a suitable match for the heir to the Austro-Hungarian throne. 'Morganatic' derives from the Old High German word *morgan* (morning), and a morganatic marriage is one in which a difference in rank leads to some rather important differences in privileges. There was no dowry for Sophie and no ownership of vast estates – only a traditional 'morning gift' from her husband. Her children would not be in line to inherit the throne and she was not even permitted to sit beside her husband in the royal carriage or in the royal box at the opera.

But when Emperor Franz Josef reluctantly agreed to the marriage, nothing was said about who was permitted to sit next to whom in a car. Sophie and Franz Ferdinand were in the same open-topped car in Sarajevo, Bosnia, on 28 June 1914, when a Serbian nationalist, Gavrilo Princip, stepped forward, gun in hand, and assassinated both of them. Given the tensions that existed in the Balkans, along with the suspicions and rivalries between the Great Powers at the time, this was the spark that ignited the First World War.

Signs of the Times

The First World War (1914–18)
and the Treaty of Versailles (1919)

What was described, over optimistically, as 'the war to end all wars', called for new tactics and new weapons. The 1919 Treaty of Versailles, following the Allied victory, changed world maps and created new countries. And life went on, with its new fashions, new discoveries and an inevitable expansion of knowledge and new words and phrases:

Creeping barrage, tank, shell shock, gas mask, camouflage, refugee, demob, conscientious objector, Czechoslovakia, Kenya, birth control, film star, traffic jam, Bolshevik, imperialism, racialist, introvert, extrovert.

Medical Matters

A The study of the causes, consequences and treatments of disease.

B The study of abnormalities and diseases of the heart.

C The study of bones and the skeleton, intending to solve or alleviate problems.

D The branch of medicine concerned with hearing defects.

E Branch of surgery concerned with providing man-made substitutes for parts of the body.

F Suffering from an unduly severe emotional state, such as depression, anxiety or hysteria, for which there is no apparent physical cause.

G Excessive swelling in the wall of an artery, rather like a blowout on a bicycle inner tube.

H A common cause of heart attacks, resulting from the blockage of an artery carrying blood to the heart.

I The pigment that carries oxygen in red blood cells and gives the blood its colour.

J An irregular heartbeat.

Clues

A 9 letters: *pat------*

B 10 letters: *car-------*

C 9 letters: *ost------*

D 9 letters: *aud------*

E 11 letters: *pro--------*

F 8 letters: *neu-----*

G 8 letters: *ane-----*

H 2 words, 8 letters and 10: *cor----- thr-------*

I 11 letters: *hae--------*

J 2 words: 6 letters and 12: *at---- fib--------*

See.page 146 for answers

Answers, Word Origins and Usage

A **Pathology**. *Adj:* **pathological**. *Practitioner:* **pathologist**. Greek *pathos* (suffering, study of the passions) + *logos* (word). Pathological can also mean 'unhealthy, undesirable': a pathological hatred of foreigners.

B **Cardiology**. *Adj:* **cardiological**. *Practitioner:* **cardiologist**. Greek *kardia* (heart).

C **Osteology**. *Adj:* **osteological**. *Practitioner:* **osteologist**. Greek *osteon* (bone).

D **Audiology**. *Adj:* **audiological**. *Practitioner:* **audiologist**. Latin *audire* (to hear). Memory-jogger: audio.

E **Prosthetics**. *Practitioner:* **prosthetist**. Greek *prosthesis* (an addition). Fitted with prosthetic legs after his flying accident, Douglas Bader was able to achieve a respectable score on the golf course.

F **Neurotic**. *Nouns:* **neurosis, neuroses, neuroticism**. Greek *neuron* (nerve).

G **Aneurism**. Greek *ana* (throughout) + *eurunein* (to dilate).

H **Coronary thrombosis**. Latin *corona* (garland, crown) + *thrombos* (a clot). The medical term for a heart attack is **myocardial infarction**.

I **Haemoglobin**. Greek *haimato* (blood).

J **Atrial fibrillation**. An **atrium** is an upper chamber of the heart. Latin *fibril* (fibre). There is a twitching of individual fibres rather than movement of the heart muscle as a whole.

Complementary Medicine

A Therapies that take into account the health of the entire body rather than concentrating on individual symptoms.

B The massaging of different areas of the feet to cure disorders in other parts of the body.

C The application of heat to the body to stimulate the flow of vital energy and so effect a cure.

D A therapy based on the idea that a miniscule, much diluted, amount of something that is normally harmful will stimulate the body's immune system into action and so be beneficial.

E The study and manipulation of bones.

F A method of improving posture as a way of helping the body to relax and work more efficiently.

G A system of exercises stressing the importance of muscle control, correct breathing and the correct alignment of the spine.

H A method designed to fend off illness and restore good health by taking preparations created from flowers and plants, diluted with spring water.

I The use of scientific measuring equipment to train a patient to become aware of and establish an element of control over what are normally automatic and unconscious processes taking place within the body.

J A therapy based on the manipulation of poorly aligned joints.

Clues

A 8 letters: *hol-----*

B 11 letters: *ref--------*

C 11 letters: *mox--------*

D 10 letters: *hom-------*

E 10 letters: *ost-------*

F 2 words, 9 letters each: *Ale------ Tec------*

G 7 letters: *Pil----*

H 2 words, 4, 6 and 8 letters: *B--- Fl---- Rem-----*

I 11 letters: *bio--------*

J 12 letters: *chi---------*

See page 148 for answers

Answers, Word Origins and Usage

A **Holistic**. *Noun:* **holism**. Greek *holos* (whole). The word is also used in non-medical contexts: This is a bigger problem than we thought, so we had better take a holistic view.

B **Reflexology**. *Practitioner:* **reflexologist**. The theory is that different organs of the body will respond, with no conscious effort but in a reflex way, to stimulation of different areas of the feet.

C **Moxibustion**. This therapy, in which plant leaves are burned near affected areas, originated in Asia, where the leaves used were those of the *Artemisia moxa* plant. Memory-jogger: combustion.

D **Homeopathy**. *Adj:* **homeopathic**. *Practitioner:* **homeopath**. Greek *homos* (the same).

E **Osteopathy**. *Adj:* **osteopathic**. *Practitioner:* **osteopath**. Greek *osteon* (bone).

F **Alexander Technique**. Named after the Australian-born actor Frederick Matthias Alexander (1869–1955) who began to lose his voice on stage but recovered it after he worked out ways of improving his posture.

G **Pilates**. Named after Joseph Pilates (1883–1967), a German-born gymnast, bodybuilder and boxer who developed a system of fitness exercises while he was interned in Britain during the First World War.

H **Bach Flower Remedies**. Based on the experiments and findings of the English physician Edward Bach (1889–1936).

I **Biofeedback**. Greek *bios* (human life).

J **Chiropractic**. Greek *kheir* (hand) + *praktikos* (practical). Not to be confused with **chiropody**, the care of the feet.

Signs of the Times

The Roaring Twenties

On the surface it looked as if one of the main purposes in life during the 1920s was simply to have fun. But over the horizon some sinister-looking clouds were gathering. The following are among terms that came into everyday usage:

Bathing beauty, cocktail party, sunbathing, flapper, naturist, birth control, Charleston (dance), face-lift, superstar, sex symbol, T-shirt, hitch hike, Soviet, Fascist, Blackshirt, National Socialist, liquidate, robot, fundamentalism, totalitarianism, collective farm, isolationism, means test, recession, service charge, intelligence test, inferiority complex, id, pecking order, transvestite, zip fastener, aerosol, motel, traffic lights, assembly line, public relations, insulin, penicillin, oestrogen, Surrealism.

Drek, Schlep and Schmaltz

Does any language in the world do a better job than Yiddish of linking the sound of a word to its meaning? It is highly unlikely. This expressive and onomatopoeic tongue, a blend of Germanic, Hebrew and Slavonic, has spread wherever Jewish communities have settled. *Drek* means vulgar, rubbishy and worthless. To *schlep* means to shuffle along wearily, carrying a burden that is as awkward as it is heavy. A *shmuck* is clumsy, tactless and thick-witted. And *schmaltz* says all that needs to be said about sentimentality that has become cloyingly excessive. Among other Yiddish words that echo their meaning in sound are: *chutzpah* – audacity, cheek, nerve; *kvetch* – to moan, and complain without respite; *nebbish* – a nobody, somebody who keeps to the fringes of life and makes no impression; stay *shtum* – to keep one's mouth shut; *schnozzle* – the nose, especially a prominent one; and *nudnik* – a pain in the neck.

This is not to say that every Yiddish word combines meaning and sound, but the language of the *shtetl* (a pre-holocaust Jewish settlement in Eastern Europe) is always lively and colourful. Take, for example: *mensch* – an upright, honest man; *meshuga* – mad, crazy; *latke* – a potato pancake; *maven* – an expert or connoisseur; *shiksa* – a non-Jewish girl; *goy* – a gentile; *kibbutz* – a collective farm where volunteers help to turn the desert green; *kibitz* – to offer unwanted advice, originally at a card game but now in any situation; *gonef* – a thief; *tush* – backside; *schemozzle* – brawl, confusion, and *Mazel tov!* – Congratulations!

The Latin Prefix In-

A A built-in aspect of the essential nature of whatever is being discussed or considered.

B Tiny crevices, cracks or holes.

C So extreme, so overwhelming or in some instances so sacred that it cannot be put into words.

D A blood-red colour.

E To break into a conversation with one's own views; insert words into a book or other printed matter.

F Refusing to give way in a dispute; uncompromising.

G Much given to the contemplation of one's own thoughts and feelings.

H In grammar, a verb that does not take a direct object.

I An ingrained strand in a person's character; a firmly rooted habit.

J The other person in a conversation.

Clues

A 9 letters: *int*------

B 11 letters: *int*--------

C 9 letters: *ine*------

D 11 letters: *inc*--------

E 11 letters: *int*--------

F 12 letters: *int*---------

G 13 letters: *int*----------

H 12 letters: *int*---------

I 10 letters: *inv*-------

J 12 letters: *int*---------

See page 152 for answers

Word Origins and Usage

A **Intrinsic**. *Adv:* **intrinsically**. Latin *intrinsecus* (inward). Example: It was an intrinsic part of Janet's nature that she always trusted people, no matter how many times she had been let down.

B **Interstices**. *Adj:* **interstitial**. Latin *inter* (between) + *sistere* (to stand). Example: The net was badly in need of repair because most of the interstices had come loose with age.

C **Ineffable**. *Noun:* **ineffability**. *Adv:* **ineffably**. Latin *in* (not) + *effari* (utter). Example: My mother beamed with ineffable delight when Kirstie, her Scottie dog, won the title 'Best in Show'.

D **Incarnadine**. *Verb:* same spelling as the adjective. Italian *incarnadino* (flesh-coloured). Lady Macbeth, in the sleepwalking scene from Shakespeare's play, fears there is so much blood on her hands that if she tried to wash it away it would 'the multitudinous seas incarnadine'.

E **Interpolate**. *Noun:* **interpolation**. *Practitioner:* **interpolator**. Latin *inter* (between) + *polare* (to add, alter).

F **Intransigent**. *Nouns:* **intransigence, intransigency**. Latin *in* (not) + *transigere* (to compromise). Example: Eleven of the jury agreed on a guilty verdict but one man was intransigent and no argument could sway him.

G **Introspective**. *Noun:* **introspection**. Latin *intro* (into) + *specere* (to look).

H **Intransitive**. Latin *transire* (to go across). A **transitive** verb needs a direct object, usually a noun, in order for a sentence to make sense: the greedy man devoured ten pies. An intransitive verb has no such need: the deck chair collapsed.

I **Inveterate**. Latin *inveterare* (to make old). An inveterate supporter of lost causes. Memory-jogger: veteran.

J **Interlocutor**. Latin *inter* (between) + *loqui* (to speak). Example: My interlocutor kept interrupting with pointless questions.

Winds of the World

A   A warm, dry wind that causes a rapid rise in temperature as it blows down the eastern slopes of the Rocky Mountains.

B   A warm, dry wind that blows down the northern slopes of the Alps.

C   A strong and constant wind that drove ships through the southern oceans at a spanking pace in the age of sail.

D   A wind from the Sahara that, in its season, brings a spell of dust and dryness to the coast of West Africa.

E   A cold, dry, squally wind that blows from France's central plateau towards the Mediterranean coast.

F   A strong wind blowing at speeds of 62–74 km/h (39–46 mph) and registering Force 8 on the Beaufort scale.

G   A violently destructive wind that revolves counter-clockwise over vast sea areas in the northern hemisphere at more than 32.7 m. (107 ft 3 in.) per second, before spending out its force on land.

H   The same kind of wind as G, but revolving clockwise and in the southern hemisphere.

I   A violently revolving wind in the West Pacific.

J   A devastating, funnel-shaped column of air that swirls at up to 480 km/h (300 mph) and can uproot trees, fling cars through the air and claim human lives.

Clues

A   7 letters: *Ch-----*

B   4 letters: *F---*

C   2 words, both 7 letters: *R------ F------*

D   9 letters: *Har------*

E   7 letters: *Mis----*

F   4 letters: *g---*

G   9 letters: *hur------*

H   2 words: 8 letters and 7: *tro----- cy----*

I   7 letters: *ty-----*

J   7 letters: *to-----*

See page 154 for answers

Answers, Word Origins and Usage

A **Chinook**. Named after a local North American Indian tribe.

B **Föhn**. Germanised version of the Latin *ventus favonius* (the West Wind).

C **Roaring Forties**. So named because they begin south of the 40 degrees S. line of latitude.

D **Harmattan**. Possibly from Arabic *harama* (forbidden). Along the Gulf of Guinea the Harmattan is also known as the 'doctor wind' because its dryness brings a welcome relief from the prevailing humidity.

E **Mistral**. Latin *magistralis ventus* (the master wind).

F **Gale**. A gale blowing at 75–88 km/h (47–54 mph) and registering 9 on the Beaufort scale is termed a fresh gale. One at 89–102 km/h (55–63 mph) is a whole gale.

G **Hurricane**. Spanish *huracan*, probably a term meaning 'god of the storm', taken over by the conquistadores from a Caribbean language that has become extinct.

H **Tropical cyclone**. Probably from Greek *kuklos* (circle). A hurricane is a cyclone, spiralling counter-clockwise and in the northern hemisphere.

I **Typhoon**. Chinese (Cantonese) *daai fung* (great wind).

J **Tornado**. Amalgamation of Spanish *tornado* (turning) and *tronada* (thunderstorm). An informal U.S. term for a tornado is twister.

Animal Quackers

British ducks say *quack*, British cows *moo*, sheep *baa*, pigs go *oink-oink*, cockerels greet the dawn with *cock-a-doodle doo*, cats *miaow*, dogs bark *woof! woof!*, donkeys say *hee-haw* and frogs somehow manage to produce *ribbet, ribbet*. Farm animals and pets on the other side of the Channel speak a different language – except for cats, which make much the same sound as British felines but with a slight difference in spelling.

French ducks say *coin coin* (pronounced kwan kwan).
French cows say *meuh*.

French sheep go *béé béé*.

French pigs grunt *groing-groing* (grwan-grwan).

French cockerels announce a new day with *kok-oree-ko!*

French cats *miauo*.

French dogs bark *ouah! ouah!*

French donkeys say *hi-haur* (the *h* is silent).

French frogs go *croa-croa*.

Signs of the Times

The Thirties (1930–39)

This decade became known as 'The Hungry Thirties' because the economic depression still lingered. But life had its compensations too, with an upsurge of home comforts becoming available for those who could afford them and entertainment for all, through wireless, the cinema and sport. In the background – and pushing its way into the foreground as the decade approached an end – was the growing threat of a new outbreak of war. Among the words that made their appearance in the Thirties are:

Depression, New Deal, green belt, garden city, Belisha beacon, supermarket, garden city, polio, iron lung, crooner, bingo, brains trust, bodyline, cheesecake, Oscar, VIP, striptease, colour supplement, crew cut, jive, juke box, glamour boy, teenager, supermarket, air conditioning, electric blanket, tape recorder, fruit machine, Nazi, swastika, Gestapo, SS, New Order, fifth column, Bren gun, dive-bomber, blitz, radar, evacuee, blackout, witch hunt, rat race.

Signs of the Times

The Second World War and Austerity (1939–50)

One of the major differences between the two World Wars fought by Britain in the twentieth century was that in the second, the entire civilian population was in the front line. Their courage in the face of this grim experience is reflected in the words and slogans of the time. The war years also saw an influx of Americans and Americanisms. William Connor, star columnist of the *Daily Mirror*, who had other things to do during the war, made the best 'outbreak of peace' joke: 'As I was saying, before I was so rudely interrupted...'

Victory was followed by austerity rather than by prosperity. The war was over, but bread was rationed for the first time and until March 1949 clothing could not be bought without handing over coupons. Against that, Clement Attlee's government introduced a welfare state, with the National Health Service in pride of place. British inventors, who had performed to great effect during the war, remained as inventive as ever. Words and phrases that came to the fore include:

Ack Ack, blitzkrieg, Anderson shelter, Morrison shelter, Britain can take it, careless talk costs lives, dig for victory, paratroops, the forgotten army, quisling, collaborator, flying bomb, V2, British restaurant, fraternisation, bouncing bomb, jet engine, genocide, boffin, brain drain, atom bomb, fusion, national service, National Health Service, welfare state, comprehensive schools, holiday camp, youth club, pin-up, bikini, jitterbugging, GI brides.

It Takes All Kinds

A   A person of taste who dabbles in the fine arts, rather than adopting the more painstaking approach of a true connoisseur.

B   In two minds, uncertain, evasive.

C   Speaking only one language.

D   Unique; so unusual as to be beyond imitation.

E   Insipid, soothing, intended to avoid causing offence.

F   Attractive at first sight but cheap and tawdry on closer scrutiny.

G   An outcome that depends on luck, chance or choices made at random.

H   Something that is placed in the wrong historical time.

Clues

A   10 letters: *dil*-------

B   9 letters: *equ*------

C   8 letters: *mon*-----

D   10 letters: *ini*-------

E   7 letters: *ano*----

F   12 letters: *mer*---------

G   8 letters: *ale*-----

H   11 letters: *ana*--------

See page 158 for answers

Answers, Word Origins and Usage

A **Dilettante**. *Adj:* **dilettantish**. *The practice:* **dilettantism**. *Plurals:* **dilettanti**, **dilettantes**. Italian for 'amateur'.

B **Equivocal**. *Verb:* **equivocate**. Latin *equi* (equal) + *vox* (voice).

C **Monoglot**. From the Greek for 'single-tongued'.

D **Inimitable**. Memory-jogger: beyond imitation.

E **Anodyne**. Also **anodynic**. Latin *anodynus* (painless). Example: A recorded message came out with the usual anodyne excuse for delay: 'Your call is important to us.'

F **Meretricious**. Latin *meretrix* (a prostitute). Example: I've heard enough of your meretricious schemes for making a fortune, so why don't we stay with something that's less ambitious but within the law?

G **Aleatory**. Latin *aleator* (gambler, dice thrower). Example: The pianist gave, as an encore, a brilliant aleatory performance based on a Schumann song.

H **Anachronism**. *Adjs:* **anachronistic**, **anachronous**. Greek *ana* (backwards) + *khronos* (time). Television producers have to be on constant watch against such anachronisms as wristwatches peeping out from under the sleeves of actors in a Jane Austen series.

Signs of the Times

The Fifties (1950–59)

Austerity… scrimping and scraping… deference to authority… teenagers beginning to reject the ambitions and styles of their parents… the shadow of the atomic bomb, but at the same time, great expectations for the future. The Fifties were a generational crossroads, offering a choice between hanging on to the copybook maxims of behaviour and throwing off restrictions and inhibitions. Words that entered the language or took on new meanings:

Beatnik, hippie, Teddy boy, hit parade, skiffle, hi-fi, rock 'n' roll, boutique, angry young man, pop art, meritocracy, Big Bang (theory about the origins of the universe), flying saucers, UFOs, Sputnik, cosmonaut, brainwashing, double helix, transplant, the pill, thalidomide, DIY, fast food, video, Xerox.

Buildings, Sacred and Secular

A   A projecting shelf on the underside of a hinged seat, which offers the support of allowing a weary participant to lean back and half-sit, half-stand during a long church service.

B   An arch-shaped structure supporting a wall and helping to carry the weight of the roof.

C   A carved screen behind a church's altar.

D   The privy in a monastery or convent.

E   A Gothic style of church building in England during the thirteenth and fourteenth centuries, with elaborate stonework in windows and arches.

F   A slit in the wall of a castle tower, through which an archer could fire down on attackers.

G   A painting made on fresh plaster, with the colours setting as it dries out.

H   A decorated horizontal band, high on the front of a building or on the wall of a room.

I   The main front of a building.

J   A pillar carved in the shape of a draped female figure who appears to be bearing the weight of a temple's roof on her head.

Clues

A   10 letters: *mis-------*

B   2 words, 6 letters and 8: *fl---- but-----*

C   7 letters: *rer----*

D   10 letters: *rer-------*

E   9 letters: *dec------*

F   9 letters: *emb------*

G   6 letters: *fr----*

H   6 letters: *fr----*

I   6 letters: *fa----*

J   8 letters: *car-----*

See page 160 for answers

Answers, Word Origins and Usage

A **Misericord**. Latin *misericordia* (compassionate, to show pity).

B **Flying buttress**. Old French *bouterez* (to strike against, thrust against).

C **Reredos**. Old French *arere* (behind) + *dos* (back).

D **Reredorter**. Also known as 'house of ease'.

E **Decorated**.

F **Embrasure**. French *embraser* (to set on fire).

G **Fresco**. Italian for 'fresh'.

H **Frieze**. Latin *frisium* (embroidered fringe).

I **Façade**. Probably from Latin *facia* (face). The word can also mean 'a misleading presentation, a false front, put on to deceive'.

J **Caryatid**. Greek *karuatides* (priestesses of the virgin goddess Artemis).

Names into Words

When the Greek god Apollo clapped eyes on Cassandra, daughter of King Priam of Troy, it was a case of lust at first sight. She was so beautiful that Apollo decided to woo her with an exceptional present. He gave her the gift of prophecy. But while Cassandra took the gift she turned down the giver, Apollo, who – unused to receiving 'No' as an answer – put a curse on her: she could prophesy as much as she liked but nobody would believe her.

When the Greeks, after ten years of fighting, left a wooden horse outside the gates of Troy and pretended to set sail for home, Cassandra forecast doom if it were taken into the city. Partly out of natural curiosity and partly because of Apollo's curse, the Trojans spurned Cassandra's heartfelt warnings. They trundled the horse into their city, with hand-picked Greek warriors crouched inside its belly. When night came, the Greeks scrambled out to kill the guards and open the city gates. Troy fell, its towers were burned and most of its defenders slain or enslaved. The legend is remembered every time the epithet **Cassandra** is applied to somebody who has a reputation for moaning, bewailing and always expecting the worst.

Buildings, Sacred and Secular

A Hard, brownish-red mixture, mainly of sand and clay, used in pottery and as decoration in buildings.

B Roman system of underfloor heating.

C Grotesque and terrifying figure at the head of a spout carrying rainwater away from the roof of a mediaeval building.

D A style of English architecture and furniture associated with the reign of James I (1603–25).

E A steep-sided roof, French in origin, with space for a room inside rather than beneath.

F Style of architecture of the late eleventh and twelfth centuries, with pointed arches and dogtooth carving on pillars.

G A high four-sided stone pillar, coming to a point at the top, and acting as a commemorative landmark.

H A projecting upper-storey window.

I An elaborate, ornate style in architecture, music and painting, popular in Europe from the late sixteenth century to the early eighteenth.

J A highly elaborate style of architecture, with a profusion of curves and flourishes, that captivated a fair number of European countries from *c.* 1720–75 but has been criticised for its over-sweetness.

Clues

A   10 letters: *ter*-------

B   9 letters: *hyp*------

C   8 letters: *gar*-----

D   8 letters: *Jac*-----

E   7 letters: *man*----

F   6 letters: *N*-----

G   7 letters: *obe*----

H   5 letters: *or*---

I   7 letters: *bar*----

J   6 letters: *roc*---

See page 162 for answers

Answers, Word Origins and Usage

A **Terracotta**. Italian for 'baked earth'.

B **Hypocaust**. Greek *hupo* (underneath) + *kaiein* (to burn).

C **Gargoyle**. Latin *gurgulio* (throat, windpipe).

D **Jacobean**. Latin *Jacobus* (James).

E **Mansard**. Named after its designer, the French architect François Mansart (1598–1666).

F **Norman**.

G **Obelisk**. Greek *obeliskos* (pointed pillar). Cleopatra's Needle is a famous obelisk.

H **Oriel**. Old French *oriol* (gallery).

I **Baroque**. From the Portuguese *barroco*, a pearl with an unusual shape.

J **Rococo**. Derived from the French *rocaille*, a style based on seashells.

Signs of the Times

The Sixties (1960–69)

Harold Macmillan opened the decade with his announcement that a wind of change was sweeping through Africa. The wind did not stop there. This was a decade that turned its back on the past in a search for new excitements, new prosperity and new possibilities. Among the words and phrases added to the language were:

Beatlemania, disco, groupie, the Twist, sitcom, flower children, streetwise, topless, miniskirt, transcendental meditation, game show, chat show, Daleks, golden handshake, commute, focus group, mission statement, jumbo jet, jet lag, breathalyser, identikit, pulsar, quasar, Black Hole, black power, dreadlocks, women's lib, laser beam, cassette, nuke, Wasp (White Anglo-Saxon Protestant), genetic engineering, homophobia, digital, database, byte, mouse (for a computer).

Buildings, Sacred and Secular

A   One of the three classical Orders of Greek architecture, characterised by the depiction of acanthus leaves at the tops of columns.

B   One of the three classical Orders of Greek architecture, characterised by scrolls at the tops of columns.

C   One of the three classical Orders of Greek of architecture, characterised by heavily fluted columns, topped by plain and simple geometric shapes.

D   A fortified citadel on a commanding height overlooking a city in Ancient Greece.

E   Ancient Greek or Roman open-air theatre, circular or oval, with seats rising in tiers.

F   A spacious entrance hall, often rising for several storeys and with an open or glazed roof. Originally the central court in a Roman house.

G   Chamber with a large hot-water bath in a Roman bathhouse.

H   Chamber with a large cold-water bath in a Roman bathhouse.

I   Covered arcade round an open court in a monastery or college.

Clues

A   10 letters: *Cor*-------

B   5 letters: *I*----

C   5 letters: *D*----

D   9 letters: *acr*------

E   12 letters: *amp*---------

F   6 letters: *at*----

G   9 letters: *cal*------

H   11 letters: *fri*--------

I   8 letters: *clo*-----

See page 164 for answers

Answers, Word Origins and Usage

A **Corinthian**. Associated with the city state of Corinth. The style was much used by the Romans.

B **Ionic**. From the chain of islands in Greece's Ionic Sea.

C **Doric**. This is one of the four main dialects of Ancient Greece.

D **Acropolis**. Greek for 'upper city'. The Acropolis overlooking Athens is the site of the **Parthenon** temple.

E **Amphitheatre**. Greek *amphi* (around, on all sides).

F **Atrium.** Origin uncertain. *Plurals:* both *atriums* and *atria* are acceptable.

G **Caldarium**. Latin *calidus* (hot).

H **Frigidarium**.

I **Cloister**. Latin *claustrum* (lock, enclosed space).

Behind the Word

Proteus was a Greek god who had the handy knack of being able to confuse and ward off bothersome questioners by changing his shape. His name lives on in the protea, a flower that presents itself in a kaleidoscope variety of colours, and in the word **protean** – applied to anything that is constantly subject to change.

Buildings, Sacred and Secular

A A summer house or open gallery, built on a site that gives access to a fine view.

B Ornate decoration using swirling geometric patterns and often fruit or flowers, but never images of humans or animals.

C A fortified structure outside a town or castle, especially one built to defend a gate or drawbridge.

D A mock ruin or a building that is not meant to be lived in but is placed in the grounds of a stately home to lend an air of romance.

E Originally, a temple dedicated to the gods; now also used to mean 'a group of heroes and others deserving of fame'.

F A section jutting out from any structure and supported at only one end. Often used in bridge construction.

G A type of window that opens and shuts on hinges.

H A pyramid built by ancient Syrians and Babylonians, with a succession of storeys, each smaller than the one beneath.

I A bell tower, built close to but apart from its parent church.

J A small dome, crowning a larger dome.

Clues

A 9 letters: *bel------*

B 9 letters: *Ara------*

C 8 letters: *bar-----*

D 5 letters: *f----*

E 8 letters: *pan-----*

F 10 letters: *can-------*

G 8 letters: *cas-----*

H 8 letters: *zig-----*

I 9 letters: *cam------*

J 6 letters: *cu----*

See page 166 for answers

Answers, Word Origins and Usage

A **Belvedere**. Italian for 'beautiful view'.

B **Arabesque**. Italian *arabesco* (Arab-style).

C **Barbican**.

D **Folly**.

E **Pantheon**. Greek *pan* (all) + *theos* (god). Example: He may have upset many opponents with his paranoid suspicions but nobody can deny that Bobby Fischer deserves his place in the pantheon of great chess players.

F **Cantilever**. *Memory-jogger:* counterbalance.

G **Casement** window. *Adj:* **casemented**.

H **Ziggurat**. Assyrian *zaqaru* (high).

I **Campanile**. Italian *campana* (bell). *Bellringer:* **campanologist**.

J **Cupola**. Latin for 'a small cask'.

Signs of the Times

The Seventies (1970–79)

The Swinging Sixties gave way to the Serious Seventies, a time of industrial strife, increasing financial worries and, in Northern Ireland, of increasing violence. There were still, however, some lighter touches. New words and phrases:

No-go-area, kneecapping, Exocet, quango, industrial action, downsize, flying picket, gentrify, poverty trap, global warming, political correctness, single currency, debit card, sell-by date, whistleblower, -gate (as in Watergate), bulimia, legionnaires' disease, junk food, passive smoking, nouvelle cuisine, Beaujolais Nouveau Race, hard disk, floppy disk, computer virus, user-friendly, laser printer, boat people, global warming, hot pants, streaking, baby boomer, megastar, Sloane Ranger, Page Three Girl, punk rock, action replay, bungee jumping.

Digging Up the Past

A   A prehistoric burial mound, covered with earth or stones.

B   Ancient dwelling, usually fortified, on a lake or swampy land.

C   A circle of upright stones, surrounding a mound.

D   A single large stone, placed upright.

E   An ancient tomb, formed by two or more upright stones, supporting a stone roof.

F   An exceptionally large stone, used in prehistoric monuments.

G   The Old Stone Age, when humans began to use chipped tools.

H   The New Stone Age, when hunting and gathering were gradually replaced by farming.

I   A method of dating by examining the rings in trees.

J   A pillar or upright slab, with decorations or inscriptions carved on the surface.

Clues

A   6 letters: *b*-----

B   7 letters: *cr*-----

C   8 letters: *cr*------

D   8 letters: *mo*------

E   6 letters: *do*----

F   8 letters: *meg*-----

G   12 letters: *Pal*---------

H   9 letters: *neo*------

I   16 letters: *den*-------------

J   5 letters: *st*---

See page 168 for answers

Answers, Word Origins and Usage

A **Barrow**. *Alternative name:* **tumulus**.

B **Crannog**. Old Irish *crann* (timber).

C **Cromlech**.

D **Monolith**. *Adj:* **monolithic**. Greek *mono* (single, alone) + *lithos* (stone).

E **Dolmen**.

F **Megalith**. *Adj:* **megalithic**. Greek *megas* (great) + *lithos* (stone).

G **Palaeolithic**. Greek *palaois* (long ago) + *lithos* (stone).

H **Neolithic**. Greek *neos* (new) + *lithos* (stone).

I **Dendrochronology**. Greek *dendron* (tree).

J **Stele**. Latin *stela* (pillar).

Names into Words

The Old Testament prophet Jeremiah saw much to denounce in the Jerusalem of his day. Here are some of his powerfully expressed lamentations:

'Remembering mine affliction and my misery, the wormwood and the gall'... 'It is good for a man that he bear the yoke in his youth'... 'The heart is deceitful above all things and desperately wicked'... 'Behold, I will make thee a terror to thyself and to all thy friends'... 'Can the Ethiopian change his skin or the leopard his spots?'

So deep an impression did his words make that some 3,000 years after his death, anybody who acquires a reputation for moaning and complaining is called a **Jeremiah**, and an especially bitter complaint is termed **Jeremiad**.

Sport in Spain

Bullfighting is not to everybody's taste, but if you want to read or re-read Hemingway in his heyday you will need some acquaintance with the language of the arena of blood and sand.

A   A knowledgeable devotee of the bullfight.

B   A decorated dart, thrown into the neck or shoulder of a fighting bull to weaken it.

C   A bullfight.

D   The bullfighter.

E   A horseman armed with a lance, whose job it is to bring the bull's head low.

F   A bullfighter or a member of his team.

G   A short, red-coloured cape, flourished by the bullfighter and used to make graceful passes as it is charged by the bull.

H   A pass in which the bullfighter is stationary, moving his cape aside at the last possible moment, so that the horns of the charging bull sweep very close to his body.

I   The moment when the bullfighter makes his final sword thrust, with the objective of making a quick, clean kill.

Clues

A   10 letters: *afi-------*

B   10 letters: *ban-------*

C   7 letters: *cor----*

D   7 letters: *m------*

E   7 letters: *pic----*

F   6 letters: *to----*

G   6 letters: *mu----*

H   8 letters: *ver-----*

I   4 words, 3, 6, 2 and 5 letters: *t-- m----- o- t----*

See page 170 for answers

Answers, Word Origins and Usage

A **Aficionado**. Spanish *aficioner* (to grow fond of).

B **Banderilla**. *The thrower:* **banderillero**. Spanish *bandera* (banner).

C **Corrida**. Spanish *correr* (to run). Memory-jogger: courier.

D **Matador**. Spanish *matar* (to kill).

E **Picador**. Spanish *picar* (to pierce).

F **Torero**. Latin *taurus* (a bull).

G **Muleta**. Spanish for 'crutch'.

H **Veronica**. After the girl's name.

I **The moment of truth**. From its origins in the bullring the phrase has come to be applied to a test at a time of crisis that will reveal the inner strength or weakness of the person being tested.

Signs of the Times

The Eighties (1980–89)

Computers became part of just about everyone's daily life, and the vocabulary associated with them grew apace. Supermarkets continued to change shopping habits, while politics went through a murky phase. Whether justified or not, there was a perception that the streets in towns and cities were becoming less safe. And Britain went to war over the Falklands. Among the new words and phrases:

Internet, download, reboot, (computer) icon, laptop, hacker, e-mail, loyalty card, credit card, smart card, pin number, cashback, street cred, ghetto blaster, stalker, road rage, hip hop, moonwalking, breakdancing, wicked (meaning 'outstandingly good'), pants (meaning 'bad'), glass ceiling, nimby (Not In My Back Yard), yuppie, wannabe, toy boy, bog standard, spin doctor, anorak (boring person), Aids, HIV, Botox, mad cow disease, Prozac, chattering classes, Big Bang (on the Stock Exchange), yomping.

Volcanoes and Earthquakes

A   The study of earthquakes.

B   A point on the Earth directly above the centre of an earthquake.

C   A scale used to indicate the magnitude of an earthquake.

D   A scale used to indicate the intensity of an earthquake.

E   A smaller earthquake that may follow a much larger one.

F   A gigantic wave that is set in motion by an undersea earthquake.

G   Molten rock, hurled out from a volcano when it erupts and forming lava when it cools and solidifies.

H   Large crater at the top of a volcano.

I   Rock and rocky fragments thrown out when a volcano erupts.

J   The point at which an earthquake originates.

Clues

A   10 letters: *sei-------*

B   9 letters: *epi------*

C   2 words, 7 letters and 5: *R------ s----*

D   3 words, 8, 8 and 5 letters: *Mod----- Mer----- s----*

E   10 letters: *aft-------*

F   7 letters: *t------*

G   5 letters: *ma---*

H   7 letters: *cal----*

I   2 words, 11 letters and 4: *pyr-------- r---*

J   2 words, 7 letters and 5: *se----- f----*

See page 172 for answers

Answers, Word Origins and Usage

A **Seismology**. *Adj:* **seismological**. *Practioner:* **seismologist**. Greek *seismos* (shake, earthquake).

B **Epicentre**. Greek *epi* (above, upon).

C **Richter scale**. Named after the American seismologist Charles F. Richter (1900–85).

D **Modified Mercalli scale**. The scale, which defines twelve levels of intensity, ranges from an earthquake so mild that it is hardly noticed on Earth's surface to one that causes panic and total devastation.

E **Aftershock**.

F **Tsunami**. Japanese *tsu* (port) + *nami* (wave).

G **Magma**.

H **Caldera**. Spanish for kettle.

I **Pyroclastic rock**. Greek *pur* (fire) + *klan* (to break).

J **Seismic focus**.

Signs of the Times

The Nineties (1990–99)

Computers and the Internet were making the planet a smaller place while wars, religious feuds and terrorism were making it a more dangerous one. Some new words and phrases, many of them reflecting harsher, more pessimistic attitudes:

World-wide web, dotcom, cyber café, spam (unwanted e-mails), identity theft, silver surfer, DVD...regime change, ethnic cleansing, Gulf War syndrome...New Labour, Third Way, Cool Britannia, off-message, singing from the same hymn sheet, Eurosceptic... negative equity, Black Wednesday, job seeker, laddish, trailer trash, Asbo (Anti-Social Behaviour Order)...Millennium Dome, millennium bug...Aga Saga, grunge, bling, chav, alcopop, gastropub...Viagra, Rainbow nation, Truth and Reconciliation.

Muscles and Bones

A   Either of two large fan-shaped muscles on the chest.

B   Shoulder muscle at the top of the arm.

C   Shoulder blade.

D   The lower jawbone.

E   Large triangular muscle of the back.

F   Large, flat triangular-shaped muscle of the neck and upper back.

G   Long, narrow bone to which the ribs are attached, at the front of the chest.

H   Excessive inward curvature of the lower back, associated with poor posture.

I   Excessive curvature of the upper back, often associated with weakening of the bone structure.

J   Muscles in the forearm, which move the wrist and fingers.

Clues

A   2 words, 10 letters and 5: *pe-------- m----*

B   7 letters: *de-----*

C   7 letters: *sc-----*

D   8 letters: *ma------*

E   2 words, 10 letters and 5: *lat------- d----*

F   9 letters: *tra------*

G   7 letters: *st-----*

H   8 letters: *lor-----*

I   8 letters: *kyp-----*

J   7 letters: *fl-----*

See page 174 for answers

Answers, Word Origins and Usage

A **Pectoralis major**. Latin *pectus* (breast). The **pectorals** are sometimes referred to, especially by bodybuilders, as the **pecs**.

B **Deltoid**. Latin *deltoides* (triangular).

C **Scapula**. Latin for 'shoulder'.

D **Mandible**. Latin *mandere* (to chew).

E **Latissimus dorsi**. Latin *dorsum* (the back). The paired muscles are sometimes abbreviated to the **lats**.

F **Trapezius**. Greek *trapeza* (table).

G **Sternum**. Greek *sternon* (breast, breastbone).

H **Lordosis**. Latin *lordos* (bent backwards).

I **Kyphosis**. Greek *kuphos* (bent).

J **Flexors**. Latin *flexere* (to flex).

Headlines Make the News

Since the early 1900s newspapers have devised their own language, known as *headlinese*, which uses monosyllabic words to convey meanings normally requiring two or three. The idea was to enable more information to be printed on a page, but the new language also gave birth to a passion for hilarious rhymes, puns and alliteration.

The American magazine *Variety* is renowned for producing one of the most famous, on 7 July 1935: Sticks Nix Hick Pix. The meaning was that the 'sticks' (slang for rural areas), 'nix' (give the thumbs-down) to 'pix' (the popular term for motion pictures), about 'hicks' (country folk).

Muscles and Bones

A   Long and powerful muscle at the front of the upper arm, which causes the arm to bend when it contracts.

B   Long muscle at the back of the upper arm, which straightens the arm when it contracts.

C   Either of the two powerful muscles of the buttocks.

D   The longest bone in the body, connecting the hip joint to the knee joint.

E   The kneecap, helping to cover and protect the knee joint.

F   The collarbone, connecting the breastbone to the shoulder blades.

G   Long bone in the forearm, on the same side as the thumb.

H   Long bone in the forearm, on the same side as the little finger.

I   Small bone at the base of the spine; the vestigial stump of a tail from the evolutionary past.

J   Small bones of the fingers, thumbs and toes.

K   Neither a muscle nor a bone, but fibrous connecting tissue in the knee that holds joints together and can be damaged by being twisted under sudden pressure, as sometimes happens in football games.

Clues

A   6 letters: *bi----*

B   7 letters: *tr-----*

C   2 words, each 7 letters: *glu---- m------*

D   5 letters: *f----*

E   7 letters: *pat----*

F   8 letters: *cl------*

G   6 letters: *ra----*

H   4 letters: *u---*

I   6 letters: *co----*

J   9 letters: *pha------*

K   2 words, each 8 letters: *cr------ li------*

See page 176 for answers

Answers, Word Origins and Usage

A **Biceps**. Latin *bi* (two) + *caput* (head). So named because it is attached to bones at two points known as 'heads'.

B **Triceps**. Latin *tri* (three) + *caput* (head). So named because it is attached to bones at three points known as 'heads'.

C **Gluteus maximus**. Greek *gloutos* (buttock).

D **Femur**. Latin for 'thigh'.

E **Patella**. Latin *patina* (*dish, plate* – its design is roughly plate-like).

F **Clavicle**. Latin *clavis* (key – its shape is roughly key-like).

G **Radius**. Latin for ' spoke, ray'.

H **Ulna**. Latin for 'elbow, arm'.

I **Coccyx**. Greek *kokkos* (cuckoo: the bone was held to have the shape of a cuckoo's beak).

J **Phalanges**. Greek *phalanx* (a formation of foot soldiers who went into battle packed closely together, with bristling spears and overlapping shields).

K **Cruciate ligament**. Latin *cruciatus* (cross-shaped) + *ligare* (to bind).

Military Matters

A   Code name for Germany's surprise attack on Russia on 22 June 1941.

B   Somebody who has, through the misfortunes of war, been uprooted from his or her homeland.

C   The expulsion from their home region of large numbers of an ethnic group by members of a country's dominant ethnic group.

D   A sequence that begins with limited intervention in an armed conflict but leads, step by step, to full-scale involvement in a war.

E   Killing or attempting to kill unpopular officers on one's own side, whose excessive zeal has put their troops in danger.

F   A small fortification outside an army's main defences, acting both as an observation post and as a breakwater against enemy attacks.

G   The unintentional killing and wounding of civilians and destruction of civilian property.

H   The unintended killing and wounding of troops on one's own side, caused by errors in identifying targets.

I   A pilotless plane, capable of firing rockets at its targets with pinpoint accuracy.

J   Code name for the Allied landings on the coasts of occupied Europe on D-Day, 6 June 1944.

Clues

A   10 letters: *Bar-------*

B   2 words, 9 letters and 6: *dis------ p-----*

C   2 words, 6 letters and 9: *e----- c---------*

D   2 words, 7 letters and 5: *m------ c----*

E   8 letters: *fra-----*

F   7 letters: *red----*

G   2 words, 10 letters and 6: *co------ da----*

H   2 words, 8 letters and 4: *fr------ f---*

I   5 letters: *d----*

J   8 letters: *O-------*

See page 178 for answers

Answers, Word Origins and Usage

A **Barbarossa**. Named after the Holy Roman Emperor Frederick I (*c.* 1123–90) who was known as Barbarossa because of his red beard. After subduing rebellious States in Italy, he led the Third Crusade, and defeated Muslims in battle.

B **Displaced person**.

C **Ethnic cleansing**.

D **Mission creep**.

E **Fragging**. The word comes from 'fragmentation bomb'.

F **Redoubt**. Latin *re* (an intensifier) + *ducere* (to lead).

G **Collateral damage**.

H **Friendly fire**.

I **Drone**.

J **Overlord**.

Signs of the Times

The Twenty-first Century

When terrorists crashed two hijacked passenger planes into New York's twin towers on 9/11, 2001, an almost universal comment was that the world would never be the same again. That prediction was right. A host of new words came into the language, many of them cleverly constructed but, as in *blamestorming*, *celebreality*, *cyberbegging*, *cadillacing* and *dataveillance*, without much staying power. A fair number of those connected with the ever-expanding world of computers made a more lasting mark, as did words connected with warfare:

Google, Twitter, blog, tweet, Kindle, podcast, iPad, iPod, iPhone, cyber bullying, internet troll...axis of evil, sex up, weapons-grade, freedom fries (chips – previously known in the U.S. as French fries)...speed dating, LipoStructure, nanosecond, sudoku, wind farms, HS2.

Military Matters

A A highly flammable composition, made from a secret formula, that was used in ancient and mediaeval times to set enemy ships ablaze.

B A German plan intended to give a swift knockout to France in the First World War before turing before turning to deal with Russia. It failed but a modified version in the Second World War led to the fall of France.

C Defiant stand during the Crimean War (1853–56) by the 93rd Sutherland Highlanders against a Russian cavalry attack.

D Code name for the British plan for airborne troops to capture the bridge at Arnhem, behind German forces, during the Second World War.

E Lightweight automatic rifle designed in the former USSR, and capable of firing 600 rounds per minute.

F Lightweight assault rifle favoured by many guerrilla movements and, during the Troubles in Northern Ireland, by the Provos (Provisional IRA).

G Firing in error on one's own troops or those of allies.

H A highly complex German coding machine, the final secrets of which were unlocked at Bletchley Park, Buckinghamshire, in 1940.

I An arrangement under which journalists are assigned to accompany a military unit.

J A fortified line, built along France's border with Germany that was firmly believed to be impregnable but, because it stopped short at the Ardennes, was swiftly bypassed by German forces in May 1940.

Clues

A 2 words, 5 letters and 4: *G---- F---*

B 2 words, 10 letters and 4: *Sch------- P---*

C 3 words: 4, 3 and 4 letters: *T--- R-- L---*

D 2 words, each 6 letters: *Ma---- Ga----*

E 11 letters: *Kal--------*

F 8 letters: *Ar------*

G 3 words, 4, 2 and 4 letters: *b--- o- b---*

H 2 words, 6 letters and 7: *E----- m------*

I 9 letters: *emb------*

J 2 words, 7 letters and 4: *Ma----- L---*

See page 180 for answers

Answers, Word Origins and Usage

A **Greek Fire**.

B **Schlieffen Plan**. Named after the German officer who developed it, Field Marshal Alfred Graf von Schlieffen (1833–1913).

C The **Thin Red Line**. The Highlanders, who wore red jackets, were so few that their line was only two men deep. The phrase is used on other occasions when outnumbered forces stand firm and win.

D **Market Garden**. The battle, in September 1944, was heroic but it ended in a heavy defeat for the paratroops.

E **Kalashnikov**. Designed in 1947 by the Russian Mikhail Timofeyevich Kalashnikov. Also known as the **AK 47**.

F **Armalite**.

G **Blue on blue**. The firing in error by military forces on friendly troops; also known as **friendly fire**. The term drives from training exercises in which the 'goodies' wore a blue item of uniform and the 'baddies' wore red.

H **Enigma machine**.

I **Embedding**. Other meanings are the placing of an object within another, such as a post in concrete, and a mathematical term.

J **Maginot Line**. A belief, not well founded in reality, that a plan or enterprise is perfectly safe is regarded as the product of a Maginot Line mentality.

Headlines Make the News

The headline widely derided as one of the most insensitive ever written appeared on the front page of *The Sun* on 4 May 1982 following the sinking of the Argentinian warship *General Belgrano*, during the Falklands conflict. The jubilant newspaper celebrated with a jingoistic GOTCHA! Then it went on to report the deaths of 321 Argentine seamen. The editor refused to apologise despite the public outrage that followed.

GOTCHA! was repeated by *The New York Post* above a close-up photograph of the al-Qaeda leader Osama bin Laden after he was killed by elite American forces in Pakistan on 2 May 2011.

In at the Start

A   Harmful, hostile, unhelpful, not conducive.

B   Conflict that is mutually destructive because it is between two sides from the same group.

C   Rudimentary, imperfect; at an early stage of development.

D   To confine, shut in prison.

E   A demon or evil spirit, once believed to have intercourse with sleeping women.

F   A book from the early stages of printing, without the use of moveable type. Hence, anything at a primitive stage of development.

G   Beyond all possible doubt or question.

H   Beyond the possibility of being prevented, however piteous the entreaties.

I   Native to a particular country or region.

J   Poverty-stricken, needy, destitute.

Clues

A   8 letters: *ini*-----

B   11 letters: *int*--------

C   8 letters: *inc*-----

D   11 letters: *inc*--------

E   7 letters: *inc*----

F   11 letters: *inc*--------

G   11 letters: *ind*--------

H   10 letters: *ine*-------

I   10 letters: *ind*-------

J   8 letters: *ind*-----

See page 182 for answers

Answers, Word Origins and Usage

A **Inimical**. Latin *in* (not) + *amicus* (friend). Example: It has long been known that smoking is inimical to health.

B **Internecine**. Latin *inter* (between) + *necare* (to kill, slaughter). Example: The twenty-first century, ushered in with the highest of hopes, has seen far too many outbreaks of internecine warfare.

C **Inchoate**. Latin *incohare* (to begin). Example: The word took on its meaning because the work of ploughing began with fastening a strap (*cohum*) to the plough. Example: John's boss dismissed his business plan as an inchoate mess and gave him only two days to resolve its flaws.

D **Incarcerate**. *Noun*: incarceration. Latin *carcer* (prison). Example: Gandhi served several terms of incarceration.

E **Incubus**. Latin *incubare* (to lie upon). The word is also applicable to a problem that is causing worry of nightmarish proportions.

F **Incunabulum**. *Plural*: **incunabula**. Latin *cunabula* (cradle, swaddling clothes). Strictly used, the word applies only to books printed before 1501.

G **Indubitably**. *Adj*: **indubitable**. *Noun*: **indubitability**. Latin *in* (not) + *dubitare* (to doubt).

H **Inexorable**. *Noun*: **inexorability**. *Adv* inexorably. Latin *in* (not) + *exorare* (plea, entreaty).

I **Indigenous**. *Noun*: **indigenousness**. Latin *indigena* (native). Example: The oak is indigenous to most of the world's temperate zones.

J **Indigent**. *Noun*: **indigence**. Latin *indigere* (to lack). Example: Tony's friends all knew however indigent he became he was far too proud to beg.

Behind the Word

In the days when the Germans were a collection of forest-dwelling tribes, with ferocity enough to defeat the legions of Rome, they had a word for a military camp: *heriberga*. By a process akin to Chinese whispers the word shifted slightly in meaning when it was taken into Old French. An *herberge* was simply a lodging or inn, rather than a place of shelter and rest set aside for soldiers. A *herbenger* became the man providing the lodging – the innkeeper. The word never quite threw off its origins for troops need somewhere to stay and until near the end of the seventeenth century barracks were an extreme rarity in England. A *herbinger* became the man who had to go ahead of the troops and find billets, either in inns or in the private homes of reluctant and sometimes protesting families. From there it was only a short step for **harbinger** to take on its present meaning: somebody or something that gives a forewarning of an approaching event, whether it be good news or bad.

The Witty City

Liverpool has produced more than its share of great comics and Liverpudlians have been known to explain this by claiming that you have to be a comedian to live there. It would be hard to find a region that puts so much wit into its traditional sayings. No Scouser would care to 'wake up wiv a crowd around him' because this would mean he had come off second best in a fight and had been knocked unconscious. And it will be said of a man who is exceptionally tall that he could 'wind de Mersey clock'.

Pick and Mix

A   Something so old fashioned that it is often said, jokingly, to belong to a time before the Flood.

B   An overabundance; literally, a horn of plenty.

C   A thought so striking and well expressed that it ought to be carved on stone.

D   A change in one's prospects, usually one of the downs of life rather than one of the ups.

E   A mythical monster possible to imagine but not possible to create, with the head of a lion, the body of a goat and the tail of a serpent.

F   A huge beast. By inference, an enormously powerful individual or commercial company.

G   To spread awareness, publicise, make widely known.

H   Anything that appeals to or is used by ordinary people, but especially language.

I   Resembling marble in such ways as colour, hardness and solidity.

J   A critical period during events, with far-reaching consequences.

Clues

A   12 letters: *ant*---------

B   10 letters: *cor*-------

C   8 letters: *lap*-----

D   11 letters: *vic*--------

E   7 letters: *chi*----

F   8 letters: *beh*-----

G   10 letters: *pro*-------

H   7 letters: *dem*----

I   9 letters: *mar*------

J   11 letters: *cli*--------

See page 186 for answers

Answers, Word Origins and Usage

A **Antediluvian**. Latin *ante* (before) + *diluvium* (flood). Example: Poor Jenny. Her wardrobe was positively antediluvian.

B **Cornucopia**. Latin *cornu* (horn) + *copia* (plenty). A myth tells of the god Zeus tearing the horn off a goat, then cramming it with good things and returning it, by way of recompense. Memory-jogger: copious.

C **Lapidary**. Latin *lapis* (stone).

D **Vicissitude**. Latin *vicissim* (change, turn). Example: Despite being dropped from the first team the rugby stand-off shrugged off all his vicissitudes with a smile.

E **Chimera**. Greek *khimaira* (a creature part lion, part goat, part serpent). By inference, a dream or ambition incapable of being achieved.

F **Behemoth**. Hebrew for 'great beast'. Google and Facebook have both become behemoths of the computer world in just a few years.

G **Promulgate**. *Noun*: **promulgation**. Latin *pro* (forth) + *mulgere* (to milk, bring out). Word of mouth is a good way to promulgate a new product for those who do not have the money to buy advertising space.

H **Demotic**. Greek *demos* (the common people). Example: John always had demotic tastes. Even after he won the lottery his favourite meal was still fish and chips.

I **Marmoreal**. Latin *marmor* (marble). Example: I don't think your father is going to lend you enough to buy a house outright. He has just put on his marmoreal face.

J **Climacteric**. Greek *klimakter* (the rung of a ladder). Climacteric is the medical name for a woman's change of life.

Behind the Word

Edward, Prince of Wales, who in 1901 became King Edward VII, was a leader of smart society and as such was expected to be a fashion-setter. He was so satisfied with his Savile Row tailors that he gave them a royal warrant and found it natural to turn to them for ideas. In the best Savile Row tradition they rose to the occasion and created a suit with a short jacket instead of the more formal tails. The idea caught on and soon crossed the Atlantic, for one of the firm's best customers lived in Tuxedo Park, New York. Fellow members at his club liked what they saw and that is why what is known in Britain as a dinner jacket is called a **tuxedo** by Americans – or, if they want to restore a little informality to what has become undeniably formal evening wear, a **tux**.

Headlines Make the News

The most famous inaccurate headline in newspaper history, DEWEY DEFEATS TRUMAN, was splashed on the front page of the *Chicago Tribune* of 3 November 1948. It brought the paper nothing but ridicule. The editor believed the almost unanimous forecasts of pollsters and pundits, and he was desperate to be first with the result of the presidential election. So his paper announced the winner the day before it was officially proclaimed. It turned out that the pundits were wrong. New York Governor Thomas E. Dewey did not defeat the incumbent President, Harry S. Truman. A jubilant Truman was photographed waving a copy of the newspaper after his second consecutive victory was declared.

Pick and Mix

A   The attribution of human emotions and responses to animals.

B   Standing in place for somebody else, or accepting responsibility on behalf of others.

C   A word indicating that two objects, features or ideas are closely linked.

D   The depiction, through art or in other ways, of objects belonging to the real world.

E   An unfilled gap in a story or an explanation.

F   Hazy, indistinct, unclear, impossible to pin down.

G   To weaken, spoil, reduce the force of.

H   Mean, miserly, penny-pinching, reluctant to give, spend or lend.

I   A 'holier than thou' attitude; claiming to have a high moral tone but faster to condemn than to forgive or understand.

J   A compilation of best performances ideas, styles and so on.

Clues

A   16 letters: *anth*------------

B   9 letters: *vic*------

C   11 letters: *con*--------

D   7 letters: *mi*-----

E   6 letters: *la*----

F   8 letters: *neb*-----

G   7 letters: *vit*----

H   12 letters: *par*---------

I   13 letters: *sanc*---------

J   8 letters: *ecl*------

See page 190 for answers

Answers, Word Origins and Usage

A **Anthropomorphism**. *Adjs*: **anthropomorphous**, **anthropomorphic**. Greek *anthropos* (human being) + *morphoun* (to form). Example: It may seem a touch anthropomorphic, but Sarah believes that her dog not only wags his tail but smiles every time she comes home.

B **Vicarious**. Latin for 'substitute'. Memory-jogger: vicar. (In the early Church, when bishops were scarce, vicars were appointed to replace them.)

C **Concomitant**. *Noun*: **concomitance**. Latin *com* (together) + *comitari* (to agree with). In the film *Kind Hearts and Coronets*, Alec Guinness, playing a vicar, boasts that one of his church windows has 'all the exuberance of Chaucer, without his concomitant vulgarity'.

D **Mimesis**. Greek *mimeisthai* (imitation).

E **Lacuna**. *Plural:* **lacunae**. Latin *lacuna* (lake). In F. Scott Fitzgerald's *The Great Gatsby* the exact source of Gatsby's immense wealth remains a lacuna to the end.

F **Nebulous**. *Alternative adj:* **nebular**. Latin *nebula* (a cloud). Example: Although Piers left university with a good degree, his future was nebulous.

G **Vitiate**. *Noun:* **vitiation**. Latin *vitium* (defect). Example: The disclosure that he had a criminal record rather vitiated Mark's chances of being made Chief Financial Officer.

H **Parsimonious**. *Noun:* **parsimony**. Latin *parcere* (to be sparing).

I **Sanctimonious**. *Noun:* **sanctimony**. Latin *sanctus* (sacred).

J **Eclectic**. *Noun:* **eclecticism**, Greek *ex* (out of) + *legein* (to choose). Example: After playing ten rounds in an eclectic competition, John was able to compile a 'best of the best' score which made him look like a scratch golfer.

Pick and Mix

A Reverting to an earlier, more primitive stage of life.

B Constantly hopping and flitting from one subject to another.

C Any way of doing things that has become widely accepted; a model.

D So exceptional as to seem beyond the limits of nature.

E Anything that takes place on, or is closely associated with, the banks of a river.

F One who holds a strong conviction that a church should be governed by bishops and archbishops rather than by lay members.

G A feast or any object that is splendidly lavish and wildly expensive.

H To rush about erratically, in a potentially dangerous manner, often tilting to one side.

I Linked in a series or chain of events.

J Ominous pointer to some future calamity, often used with a touch of either pomposity or humour.

Clues

A 9 letters: *ata------*

B 9 letters: *des------*

C 8 letters: *par-----*

D 13 letters: *pret---------*

E 8 letters: *rip-----*

F 12 letters: *epi---------*

G 8 letters: *Luc-----*

H 6 letters: *car---*

I 13 letters: *con----------*

J 10 letters: *por-------*

See page 192 for answers

Answers, Word Origins and Usage

A **Atavistic**. *Noun:* **atavism**. Latin *atavus* (forefather). Example: The way young Darren stuffs burgers down his mouth is positively atavistic.

B **Desultory**. *Noun:* **desultoriness**. Latin *de* (down) + *salire* (to jump). Example: If you keep shifting the focus of attention in that desultory way of yours you will never get your garden as you want it to be.

C **Paradigm**. *Adj:* **paradigmatic**. Greek *para* (side by side) + *deiknunai* (to show). Example: Dogget & Sons had been run by a member of the family ever since it was founded, but profits were falling, so it was time to bust the paradigm.

D **Preternatural**. *Adv:* **preternaturally**. Latin *praetor* (beyond) + *naturam* (nature). Example: Charlotte was only eight years old when we realised she had a preternatural gift for languages.

E **Riparian**. Latin *ripa* (bank). Example: What a pleasure it was at the weekend to put work aside and spend a riparian afternoon with nothing to do but sip wine and watch the swans and the boats go by.

F **Episcopalian**. *Alt adj:* **episcopal**. *Noun:* **episcopalianism**. Latin *episcopus* (bishop).

G **Lucullan**. Named after Lucius Lucullus, a Roman general of the first century BC, who celebrated victories with sumptuous banquets.

H **Careen**. Latin *carina* (a ship's keel – the word originates from the activity of turning a ship on to its side for repairs and cleaning).

I **Concatenation**. *Verb:* **concatenate**. Latin *catena* (chain). Example: By a concatenation of unforeseen events the night before, Larry found himself befuddled and only half sober in a bobsleigh at the top of the Cresta Run.

J **Portentous**. *Noun:* **portentousness**. *Adv:* **portentously**. *Associated verb:* **portend**. Latin *pro* (forth) + *tendere* (to stretch). Example: The minister announced, portentously, that there might have to be more cuts to the armed forces.

Pick and Mix

A   Descended from the earliest known inhabitants of a country or region; aboriginal.

B   Always ready to criticise, sit in judgement and reprimand.

C   A politician who wins popularity and moves towards power by the sheer force of his language.

D   A study that compares man-made systems, such as computers and electronics, with biological systems, such as the human brain.

E   Encountered everywhere – or seemingly everywhere.

F   Long words. And those who are fond of using them.

G   A person or character after whom something in a book, film, play, or place is named.

H   A sequence in which, as in Chinese whispers, there may be minor differences between items that are near to each other but major differences between the extremes.

I   A small group of dedicated people who share the same goals or have a common interest.

J   Giving birth to live young, which developed within the mother's body.

Clues

A   13 letters: *aut----------*

B   10 letters: *cen-------*

C   9 letters: *dem-----*

D   11 letters: *cyb--------*

E   10 letters: *ubi-------*

F   14 letters: *ses-----------*

G   9 letters: *epo------*

H   9 letters: *con—*

I   7 letters: *cot----*

J   10 letters: *viv-------*

See page 194 for answers

Answers, Word Origins and Usage

A **Autochthonous**. *Nouns*: **autochthon, autochthony**. *Adj:* **autochthonic**. Greek *autokhthon* (born from the land itself).

B **Censorious**. The censors of Ancient Rome, as well as supervising the city's census, were also responsible for overseeing morals and public behaviour.

C **Demagogue**. *Nouns:* **demagoguery, demagogy**. *Adj:* **demagogic**. Greek *demos* (the common people) + *agein* (to lead). Example: Adolf Hitler's climb to power owed much to his demagogic appeal.

D **Cybernetics**. Greek *kubernan* (to guide, steer).

E **Ubiquitous**. Latin *ubique* (everywhere). Example: The ubiquitous fried tomato is served at breakfast in just about every hotel in the land.

F **Sesquipedalian**. Latin *sesquipedalis* (a foot-and-a-half long). Example: George Orwell would not have approved. His advice was: 'Never use a long word where a short one will do.'

G **Eponymous**. Greek *epi* (to) + *onoma* (name). Example: Our daughter has been chosen to play the eponymous heroine in the school's production of *Jane Eyre*.

H **Continuum**. Latin *continuus* (continuous, held together). Example: The wages earned by professional footballers lie on a continuum between modest and astronomical.

I **Coterie**. Probably from Old French *cotier* (cottager). The overworked and overtaxed peasants of France's Ancien Régime had many common interests to draw them together.

J **Viviparous**. Latin *vivus* (alive) + *parere* (to be born).

Valley Speak

New waves in language, when they roll back into the sea, sometimes leave lasting traces on the shore and this has certainly been the case with **Valley Speak**. This manner of speaking, evolved in California's San Fernando Valley in the early Eighties, sometimes adding new words to the vocabulary and at other times commandeering existing words and increasing their circulation.

The description of anything even faintly impressive as being *awesome* is one survival from the Valley days and so is *Oh My God!*, trotted out to convey even mild levels of disgust or surprise. *Geek* and *nerd* have survived, as has *mega* for anything big. But the habit of turning every statement into a question by raising its pitch near the end is beginning to tail off. In any case, the Australians got there first.

Among the Valley words and phrases that have shown less staying power, does anybody these days summon up attention and call a group or a meeting to order by saying 'OK'? Has *totally* (pronounced *todally*) managed to elbow 'completely' aside? Is *mondo cool* still the highest praise for a boyfriend or girlfriend? The remarkable thing about Valley Speak, however, is not how much has fallen away but how much has survived. Its most lasting and most unwanted contribution has been to the misuse of the word *like*, as in: 'I was, like, have you got a new boyfriend or was that your brother last night?' Cast an eye over any of the so-called quality newspapers today and you will come cross sentences such as: 'Mo Farah dominated the 5,000 metres like he was running for sheer pleasure.' The demotic word 'like' seems be taking the rightful place of the correct but more formal 'as if'.

Headlines Make the News

Few newspapers can have blundered more sensationally than the *Christian Science Monitor* 15 April 1912. The front page declared: Passengers Safely Moved and Steamer *Titanic* Taken in Tow. All on board had survived, the *Monitor* reported. In sad reality, the death toll was 1,517 and the liner went down to its Atlantic Ocean grave.

Pick and Mix

A Behaviour, a performance or anything else that is outstandingly bad.

B Calculated to support a particular point of view; not regarded as impartial.

C Advice that is usually sound but given in a moralising, pompous way.

D Off-puttingly unattractive; aggressive and repellent.

E A long essay, arguing a case and supporting it with evidence, which is submitted by candidates for a degree or diploma.

F Plundering, despoiling, seizing without right.

G Concerned with the sense of smell.

H Spiritually uplifting, awe inspiring.

I To cause confusion, bewilder, make unintelligible, either deliberately or unintentionally.

J A statement not backed by proven evidence and so probably untrue or open to question.

Clues

A 9 letters: *egr------*

B 11 letters: *ten--------*

C 11 letters: *sen--------*

D 11 letters: *reb--------*

E 12 letters: *dis---------*

F 11 letters: *dep--------*

G 9 letters: *olf------*

H 8 letters: *num-----*

I 9 letters: *obf------*

J 10 letters: *apo-------*

See page 198 for answers

Answers, Word Origins and Usage

A **Egregious**. *Noun:* **egregiousness**. Latin *ex* (out of) + *grex* (the herd, the flock). Example: Derek's performance as the pantomime dame was egregious. Formerly, the word could also be applied to something that was outstandingly good, but this usage has fallen out of fashion.

B **Tendentious**. *Noun:* **tendentiousness**. Latin *tendere* (to stretch). Memory-jogger: Tendency.

C **Sententious**. *Noun:* **sententiousness**. Latin *sententia* (opinion).

D **Rebarbative**. Latin *barba* (beard) and Old French *rebarber.* To face an enemy, beard against beard.

E **Dissertation**. Latin *dissertare* (to discuss). Memory-jogger: Discussion.

F **Depredation**. *Adj:* **depredatory**. Latin *de* (completely) + *praedari* (to plunder).

G **Olfactory**. Latin *olere* (to smell) + *facere* (to make). Example: Hubert's olfactory nerves began working overtime the moment he crossed the threshold of his first Michelin-starred restaurant.

H **Numinous**. Latin *numen* (a nod or command from one of the gods).

I **Obfuscate**. *Noun:* **obfuscation**. Latin *obfuscare* (to darken).

J **Apocryphal**. From the *Apocrypha*, a number of books appended to the Bible that are not generally accepted as being authoritative. Greek *apokruphos* (hidden).

Headlines Make the News

One of the biggest upsets in Scottish football produced sport's most memorable headline. The unfancied Inverness team Caledonian Thistle crushed the mighty Celtic side 3-1 in the Scottish Cup in February 2000, signalling the end of manager John Barnes's reign at Celtic Park. *The Sun* headline on the match report borrowed the line 'Supercalifragilisticexpialidocious' from the 1964 Julie Andrews film *Mary Poppins* and adapted it to read: Super Caley Go Ballistic, Celtic Are Atrocious.

Pick and Mix

A   Performed in a careless, uninvolved, superficial manner.

B   Meticulous, paying scrupulous attention to every detail.

C   Unfair and likely to cause offence.

D   Promotion to the most exalted rank.

E   So fixed in one's ways as to be beyond reform or correction.

F   A subordinate who is always ready to carry out orders without question.

G   Something that causes injury or some other form of harm.

H   Likely to make matters worse, and so earning contempt or disapproval.

I   A mental process that takes place below the level of consciousness.

J   A choice between two contradictory things.

Clues

A   11 letters: *per*--------

B   11 letters: *pun*--------

C   9 letters: *inv*------

D   10 letters: *apo*-------

E   12 letters: *inc*---------

F   8 letters: *Myr*-----

G   11 letters: *dele*-------

H   10 letters: *pej*-------

I   10 letters: *sub*-------

J   9 letters: *dic*------

See page 200 for answers

Answers, Word Origins and Usage

A **Perfunctory**. *Adv:* **perfunctorily**. Latin *perfunctus* (to get through). Example: We won't use that electrician again – he made such a perfunctory job of rewiring the bathroom.

B **Punctilious**. Italian *punctiglio* (fine point). Example: Gerald is a fine workman – punctilious in every job he tackles.

C **Invidious**. Latin *invidia* (envy). Example: An invidious clause in the deed of sale meant we could not put up a shed in our own garden.

D **Apotheosis**. Greek *apo* (change) + *theos* (god). Example: Winning the 1973 Nobel Peace Prize was, at least to some, the apotheosis of Dr Kissinger's career.

E **Incorrigible**. *Noun:* **incorrigibility**. Latin *in* (not) + *corrigere* (to correct). Example: One of Henry's closest friends had the misfortune to be an incorrigible drunkard.

F **Myrmidon**. From the Greek *Murmidomes*, warriors of legendary courage, who fought under Achilles at the siege of Troy.

G **Deleterious**. Latin for 'to harm, injure'. Example: The rapidly increasing growth of supermarkets has had a deleterious effect on street corner shops.

H **Pejorative**. Latin *pejorare* (to make worse). *Associated noun:* **pejoraton**, the process of worsening. Pejorative words are left out of some dictionaries and marked 'offensive' in others.

I **Subliminal**. Latin *sub* (below) + *limen* (threshold). Example: Subliminal advertising, now illegal in Britain, attempted to sell products by flashing messages on a screen at a rate too fast to register on the conscious mind.

J **Dichotomy**. Greek *dicho* (in two parts) + *temnein* (to cut). Example: As with too many politicians, there was a marked dichotomy between his promises and his performance.

Behind the Word

A **parting shot**, if it is crushing enough, can be a deadly way of ending an argument. There was a time, though, when it was even deadlier. The ancient land of Parthia, in the northeast of today's Iran, bred a race of horsemen so skilful that when defeated in battle and in full flight they could swivel on their mounts and unleash a hail of arrows at their pursuers. This worked so well that they adopted it as a regular tactic and took their toll when only pretending to flee. The phrase 'parting shot' is a toned-down echo of *Parthian shot*.

Names into Words

The Houlihan family of the nineteenth century had an unexpected impact on the English language. Their surname is credited with being the origin of the word *hooligan*. The term first appeared in print in 1894 in court reports of a rumbustious gang, led by two Irish brothers named Houlihan, which caused mayhem in the Lambeth area of South London.

The *Oxford English Dictionary* records that 'hooligan' was also used in a music hall song of that decade which was based on the riotous behaviour of the rowdy Irish family. Arthur Conan Doyle wrote in his 1904 novel *The Adventure of the Six Napoleons* of 'an avalanche of brutality under the name of Hooliganism which has cast a dire slur on the social records of South London'. And H. G. Wells followed up in 1909 with a condemnation in his 1909 novel *Tono-Bungay* of 'three energetic young men of the hooligan type'.

Pick and Mix

A To give a rough outline; foreshadow.

B Short, sharp and overbearing.

C Diligent, taking pains to do a good job.

D Dashing, flamboyantly stylish.

E Light-hearted absence of concern for worries or danger.

F Rowdy, defiant, quick to take offence and difficult to control.

G Appropriate and fitting for a particular occasion or purpose.

H A statement, an action or a development that is threatening.

I Fortunate, favourable, advantageous.

J Lacking a definite shape.

Clues

A 9 letters: *adu------*

B 10 letters: *per-------*

C 8 letters: *sed-----*

D 7 letters: *pan----*

E 11 letters: *ins--------*

F 12 letters: *obs---------*

G 8 letters: *app-----*

H 8 letters: *min-----*

I 10 letters: *pro-------*

J 9 letters: *amo------*

See page 204 for answers

Answers, Word Origins and Usage

A **Adumbrate**. *Noun*: **adumbration**. *Adj:* **adumbrative**. Latin *adumbrare* (to overshadow). Example: It took an experienced barrister to adumbrate the main points of a weak defence case.

B **Peremptory**. *Adv:* **peremptorily**. Latin *peremptorius* (to remove the possibility of debate). Example: The sergeant major barked out his peremptory orders in a voice that could be heard beyond the barrack square.

C **Sedulous**. Latin *sedulus* (zealous). Example: Albert sedulously looked after his mother after her fall.

D **Panache**. Italian *pennachio* (a bunch of flowers worn on a hat or helmet). Example: Sir Percy Blakeney, the Scarlet Pimpernel, always brought off his rescues with plenty of panache.

E **Insouciance**. *Adj*: **insouciant**. French *in* (not) + *souciant* (to care, worry). Example: When all the others were rushing around in panic, Rupert remained as calm and insouciant as ever.

F **Obstreperous**. Latin *ob* (against) + *strepere* (to make a noise). Example: The chef was in a particularly obstreperous mood because two diners said his signature dish needed some salt.

G **Apposite**. Latin *appositus* (placed or situated near to). Example: Henrietta thought it apposite to mention on her CV that she had played hockey for Scotland.

H **Minatory**. Also **minatorial**. Latin *minari* (to menace). Example: Once Jebediah rose to his feet, with a long list of complaints, the meeting took on a minatory atmosphere.

I **Propitious**. Latin *propitius* (favourable, kindly). Example: A propitious current carried our drifting boat to a safe shore.

J **Amorphous**. Greek *amorphos* (without shape or form). Example: An amorphous figure rose from behind the gravestone, but it was only Hilary, in a white sheet, trying to scare his friends.

Acknowledgements

The following publications and electronic information providers were among the main reference sources used for checking:

The American Heritage Dictionary (Houghton Mifflin Company); Ask.com; *Bartlett's Unfamiliar Quotations*, Leonard Louis Levinson (George Allen & Unwin); *Bryson's Dictionary for Writers and Editors*, Bill Bryson (Doubleday); *Business Buzzwords*, Michael Johnson (Basil Blackwell); *The Cambridge Encyclopaedia of English*, David Crystal (Cambridge University Press); *Chambers Thesaurus*, Eds. Catherine Schwarz, Anne Seaton, George Davidson, John Simpson (Chambers); *Chambers Biographical Dictionary,* Eds. Magnus Magnusson and Rosemary Goring (Chambers); *A Dictionary of Modern Quotations*, J. M. and M. J. Cohen (Book Club Associates); *A Dictionary of Geography*, W. G. Moore (Penguin Reference Books); *A Dictionary of Modern American Usage* (OUP): *Dictionary of National Biography* (OUP); *The Etymologicon*, Mark Forsyth (Icon Books); *What Made The Crocodile Cry?* Susie Dent (OUP); *From Old English to Standard English*, Dennis Freeborn (Palgrave Macmillan); Google.com; *Idiomantics*, Philip Gooden and Peter Lewis (Bloomsbury); *The Hutchinson British/American Dictionary*, Norman Moss, (Arrow Books); *The Hutchinson Dictionary of Science*, Eds. Peter Lafferty and Julian Row (Helicon); *The language report*, Susie Dent (OUP): *It's a Wonderful Word*, Albert Jack (Arrow Books); *Reader's Digest Library of Modern Knowledge* (Reader's Digest); *Movers and Shakers*, John Ayto (OUP): *Mythology of Greece and Rome,* Arthur Cotterell (Southwater); *Oxford English Dictionary* (OUP); *The Oxford Dictionary of Modern Quotations*, Ed. Tony Augarde (OUP); *The Oxford Dictionary of Quotations* (OUP); *The Oxford English Reference Dictionary*, Eds. Judy Pearsall and Bill Trumble (OUP): *Phaidon Concise Encyclopaedia of Science and Technology*, Ed. John-David Yule (Phaidon); *The Reader's Bible*

(OUP, Cambridge University Press, Eyre and Spottiswood); *Reader's Digest Reverse Dictionary* (Reader's Digest); *Roget's II, The New Thesaurus*, Eds. of the *American Heritage Dictionary* (Houghton Mifflin Company); *Roget's Thesaurus*, Edition prepared by Susan M. Lloyd (Longman); *Reader's Digest Universal Dictionary*, Ed. Iain Redpath (Reader's Digest); *Samuel Johnson's Dictionary*, Editor Jack Lynch (Atlantic Books, London and Levenger Press, Delray Beach, Florida); *Samuel Johnson, Dictionary of the English Language*, Ed. Jack Lynch, Walker & Company; *The Secret Life of the English Language: Buttering Parsnips, Twacking Chavs*, Martin H. Manser, Associate Ed. David Pickering (Weidenfeld & Nicolson); *The Secret Life of Words*, Henry Hitchings (John Murray); *The Synonym Finder*, J. O. Rodale, revised by Laurence Urdang and Nancy Laroche (Rodale Press); *The Story of English*, Joseph Piercy (Michael O'Mara Books); *The Story of the English Language*, Mario Pei (George Allen & Unwin); *Talking for Britain*, Simon Elwes (Penguin Books); *Word Origins*, John Ayto (A & C Black); *Words, Words, Words*, David Crystal (OUP).

With special thanks to Davic MacFadyen for supplying information on the secret language of Savile Row.

Index